T0153097

Sacred ATTENTION

Sacred ATTENTION

A Spiritual Practice for Finding God in the Moment

Margaret D. McGee

Walking Together, Finding the Way®
SKYLIGHT PATHS®
PUBLISHING
Woodstock, Vermont

Sacred Attention:
A Spiritual Practice for Finding God in the Moment

2007 First Printing

Portions of this book have appeared in a slightly different form in *The Bell* (the newsletter of St. Paul's Episcopal Church in Port Townsend, Washington), *The Living Church, Alive Now*, and on the website In the Courtyard at www.inthecourtyard.com.

Some names and places have been changed.

Library of Congress Cataloging-in-Publication Data

McGee, Margaret D.
Sacred attention : a spiritual practice for finding God in the moment / Margaret D. McGee.
p. cm.
Includes bibliographical references.
ISBN-13: 978-1-59473-232-4
ISBN-10: 1-59473-232-9
1. Spiritual life—Christianity. 2. Attention—Religious aspects—Christianity. 3. Church year meditations. I. Title.

BV4501.3.M335 2007
248.4'6—dc22
2007029546

10 9 8 7 6 5 4 3 2 1

Manufactured in the United States of America
♲ Printed on recycled paper.
Jacket design: Tim Holtz
Chapter opening art: Margaret D. McGee as adapted by David H. Schroeder

SkyLight Paths Publishing is creating a place where people of different spiritual traditions come together for challenge and inspiration, a place where we can help each other understand the mystery that lies at the heart of our existence.

SkyLight Paths sees both believers and seekers as a community that increasingly transcends traditional boundaries of religion and denomination—people wanting to learn from each other, *walking together, finding the way.*

Walking Together, Finding the Way®
Published by SkyLight Paths Publishing
A Division of Longhill Partners, Inc.
Sunset Farm Offices, Route 4, P.O. Box 237
Woodstock, VT 05091
Tel: (802) 457-4000 Fax: (802) 457-4004
www.skylightpaths.com

For David

Contents

Acknowledgments

This is a short book that took a long time to write. As a result, I owe a debt of gratitude to many people—those in my thoughts today, those who've slipped out of memory, and at least a few who probably don't remember me, either. I am deeply grateful to all who played a role in the creation of this book.

My thanks to the people and clergy of St. Paul's Episcopal Church in Port Townsend, Washington, for making a spiritual home where I can grow. I'm especially grateful to The Reverend Elizabeth A. Bloch, rector at St. Paul's, for helping me see the value of this work, and to Katie Fleming, Sue Taylor, Kate Spear, Donna Cheshier, and Jeanne Dirksen of the Women's Spiritual Growth Group, who read and discussed early versions of these chapters.

Marcia Broucek pushed me to develop an idea into a manuscript, brought the proposal to the attention of SkyLight Paths, then used her fine intellect, warm spirit, and good eye to turn my manuscript into a coherent book. I'm so grateful to have Marcia as my editor and friend. At SkyLight Paths, Emily Wichland and Jessica Swift have guided both me and the book through to publication with grace, good humor, and high standards. Thank you, Emily and Jessica.

I'm fortunate to have worked with talented professional writers who challenge me to keep working until the words speak clearly. Carolyn Latteier, David Schroeder, and Janet O. Dallett gave chapters in this book the gift of their critical attention, and they have my heartfelt thanks.

Besides providing the setting for one of the chapters in this book, the Dorland Mountain Arts Colony gave me time and space to grow as a writer. I'm especially grateful to Karen Parrott and Robert Willis for helping to make my stay at Dorland productive and enriching.

I'm grateful to my family for their love and support—and also for the material.

Most of all, thanks to David, whose artful adaptation of my colored drawings made it possible for me to be both artist and author of this book, and whose love and belief in my work means more than I can say.

Introduction

SLOW DOWN—PAY ATTENTION

> 19 February.
> First salmonberry blossom. Most bushes still bare and brown, except for fat, velvety, silver-green buds at the elbows of the branches.

Shortly after my husband, David, and I moved to our house in the woods, I started to keep a nature diary. Most entries were brief, and one or two a week were plenty. My only rule was that each entry be specific to a particular plant, animal, or state of weather on a particular day.

> 4 May.
> Salmonberry bloom almost finished; a single magenta blossom left in the middle of a row of hard, green berries fuzzed with pink hairs.

Before I could describe the salmonberry bush, I had to look at it with care. I needed to be close enough to touch, smell, and, if possible, taste.

> 7 July.
> Ate thimbleberry, Pacific blackberry, and salmonberry on my walk today, each its own blend of tart, sweet, and bitter.

I started the diary to learn about the environment of my new home, and also, as a writer, to lay up professional material. My visual memory is not good. The diary would be a treasure chest that could be plundered for season-specific details any time of the year. What I did not expect was how keeping the diary would affect my prayer life. In helping me pay attention to God's work, my nature diary helped me pay attention to God. It changed the very meaning of the word *prayer* for me.

When I was about seven, my mother taught me the classic bedtime prayer, "Now I lay me down to sleep, I pray the Lord my soul to keep," followed by requests to God for blessings on family, friends, and anyone else who occurred to me at the moment. I knew then what it meant to pray—it meant talking to God. The prayers I learned by rote or made up myself, the prayers recited or heard at church, they were all messages to God. When printed on the page, a prayer looked just like a letter, starting with "Dear God" and ending with "Amen," the ecclesiastical equivalent of "Very truly yours." When said out loud, a prayer was like half of a conversation—the half in which I got to do all the talking.

Growing up, I learned about the other side of prayer—the listening side.

> God is love, and those who abide in love abide in God,
> and God abides in them.
>
> 1 JOHN 4:16

I began to understand that, if God is with us—within, among, and between every atom and being—then a conversation with God is not with a remote and distant Being, but with a fellow pilgrim. One who may be as interested in the conversation as I am.

In the best conversations, both parties listen and respond, opening up a channel of energy that flows both ways. This energy has the power to heal wounds. Spark ideas. It carries transformation in its very nature. It makes love.

Paying attention matters.

Unfortunately, paying attention does not come easy for me. I am not very good at it. Keeping a nature diary made me aware of how rarely I slowed down and looked closely at anything. When I took the time to stop, look, and listen, what I saw and heard always turned out to be unexpectedly rich. It was as if I had encountered a language both new and old, strange and familiar, prehistoric and alive. God's language. I began to wonder about all the ways that God might speak in and through creation.

Does God communicate through the natural world? Through the slug on the compost pile, the leaf on the lawn, the stone tumbled on the beach, the air that feeds my lungs, the dreams that fill my nights? How will I know unless I pay attention?

Does God communicate through my work? Through the ups and downs, the triumphs and failures, of my everyday tasks? How will I know unless I pay attention?

Does God communicate through other people? If I am made in God's image, then so is my husband, David. And so is the kind neighbor who helped us build our arbor. Oh … and that annoying co-worker who never stops talking about herself.

And so are any number of people who may strap bombs to their bodies, then try to use death to change the world. Every one of them is made in God's image. That's how they are made. Just like me.

God speaks through every single human relationship, direct or indirect. I know that. Still, it can be so difficult to pay attention.

To get better at paying attention, I needed to practice.

One summer near the end of my little brother Brian's grade school years, our father installed a basketball hoop above the garage door and spent time with each of his kids teaching us how to shoot hoops. I quickly tired of the sport, but the hoop attracted neighborhood boys, who spent long hours shooting hoops with Brian after school. They spent so much time at it, I finally asked my dad, "If practice makes perfect, why aren't any of them perfect shooters by now?"

Dad, the former high school basketball coach, answered, "They're just horsing around. You don't get better unless you practice right. Get in position, aim, follow through, watch the ball. Their shooting doesn't improve because they don't pay attention to what happens when they shoot."

To get better at paying attention, I needed to practice. And I needed to pay attention to what happened during practice.

That is what this book is all about. It tells of moments when God came knocking on the door, looking for conversation, asking for attention. Saying, "Slow down, look closely. Watch me work and see what happens."

Sometimes the process of discovery is fun. Other times it is more like peeling bandages from a wound I would rather keep hidden. The result, however, is always healing. Transforming. Writing these stories down was one way of paying attention to them. Reading the stories alone or with friends is another, sparking memories of other attention-getting moments and ideas for fresh ways to practice.

Paying attention reveals the newness of all things, so the stories in this book come from all seasons of the year. Most of them are from my own experience. A few come from people who have generously shared their stories with me. I have also drawn on scripture passages that resonate with the themes in these stories, sounding echoes of the common human experience from generations past. The writers and translators of these passages did their best to express a living relationship to God in their own words. In my writing, I generally try to avoid referring to God with gendered or hierarchical language, but things were different back then. When I read the Bible, it helps me to remember that, to the generations who come after us, we are going to sound odd in ways we can't now conceive. We can only ask that they read our words with generous hearts, looking always for the truth that lives and breathes and reaches out to new seekers through the ages.

Since I am grounded in the Episcopal tradition, I write from the Christian perspective and relate the stories to the seasons in the church's liturgical calendar. My hope is that people of all faiths will look through this lens and recognize God's universal presence.

About the Liturgical Calendar and *Sacred Attention*

Above my desk hangs a calendar that starts on January 1 and ends on December 31—one year containing twelve months. Each year of a person's life also contains twelve months, but the years are counted from birthday to birthday. And a gardener's year might start and end with the first crocus that pokes up through the last melting snow—an elastic twelve-month period that starts around the same time each year, give or take a few days.

The liturgical year of the church, like the gardener's year, is an elastic twelve months that starts around the same time each year, give or take a few days. Like the span of a person's life, the liturgical year begins in hope and expectation, with much of the high drama taking place in its first half. The second half grows from the foundation of the first, just as the second half of life grows and evolves from the choices and experience that come before it.

Over the centuries, small variations have developed among the liturgical calendars of the Eastern and Western churches and of the Protestant and Roman Catholic churches. The following overview reflects how the seasons are counted in my Episcopal church, which is typical of many Protestant denominations.

Advent	The first season in the liturgical calendar, beginning on the fourth Sunday before December 25 (around the end of November or beginning of December) and ending on Christmas Eve. Advent is a season of hope and expectation for the Incarnation of God on Earth.
Christmas season	Begins on the evening of December 24 and extends for twelve days, ending on the evening of January 5, the Eve of the Epiphany.
Epiphany	Begins on January 6 and ends on Shrove Tuesday, the last day before Lent. The term *epiphany* means a revelation of divinity or essential meaning. The Epiphany celebrates the

visit of the Magi and the recognition that Christ came to Earth for all people. (In the Roman Catholic calendar, Epiphany is celebrated as a single day, and the weeks between January 6 and Ash Wednesday are counted as the first part of Ordinary Time, continuing after the close of Easter season.)

Lent	Begins on Ash Wednesday and extends for six weeks, ending in Holy Week, the week before Easter. In some traditions, Lent ends on the eve of Maundy Thursday, the Thursday before Easter. Other traditions have Lent ending on the evening before Easter Sunday. Lent is a season of reflection and returning to God.
Easter season	Begins at sundown on the evening before Easter Sunday—the first Sunday following the first full moon after the spring equinox. The equinox usually occurs on March 21, which means the date of Easter can range between March 22 and April 25, depending on the lunar cycle. The season extends for fifty days, ending on Pentecost.
Pentecost Sunday	Marks the dividing point between the two halves of the liturgical year, occurring about six months after the start of Advent. Pentecost commemorates the coming of the Holy Spirit to the disciples after Jesus's resurrection and ascension.
Ordinary Time	Sometimes called Pentecost season, or the green season for its green liturgical color and themes of new growth. Ordinary Time makes

> up the second half of the liturgical calendar, extending from Pentecost Sunday until the start of Advent and a new liturgical year.

The twelve chapters of *Sacred Attention* follow the seasons of the liturgical calendar, from Advent through Ordinary Time. Each chapter includes a narrative, questions for reflection or discussion, suggested scripture readings, and a spiritual practice that can be used by individuals or groups. The chapters can be read in order from the beginning, or, if you prefer, you can start with the current season. For example, if your group begins *Sacred Attention* during Lent, you could start with chapter 4, "Hearty Fish Soup (Lent)," then continue through the liturgical year, circling around after chapter 12 to the first chapter and ending with chapter 3, "To See with New Eyes (Epiphany)."

The better we can pay attention, the more God meets us at every turn, asking only to be seen, smelled, tasted, touched, heard, and loved. One moment of attention turns into a prayer of power and intimacy. It is a way of prayer that can be done anytime, anywhere, as part of any activity. It has two steps.

Slow down.

Pay attention.

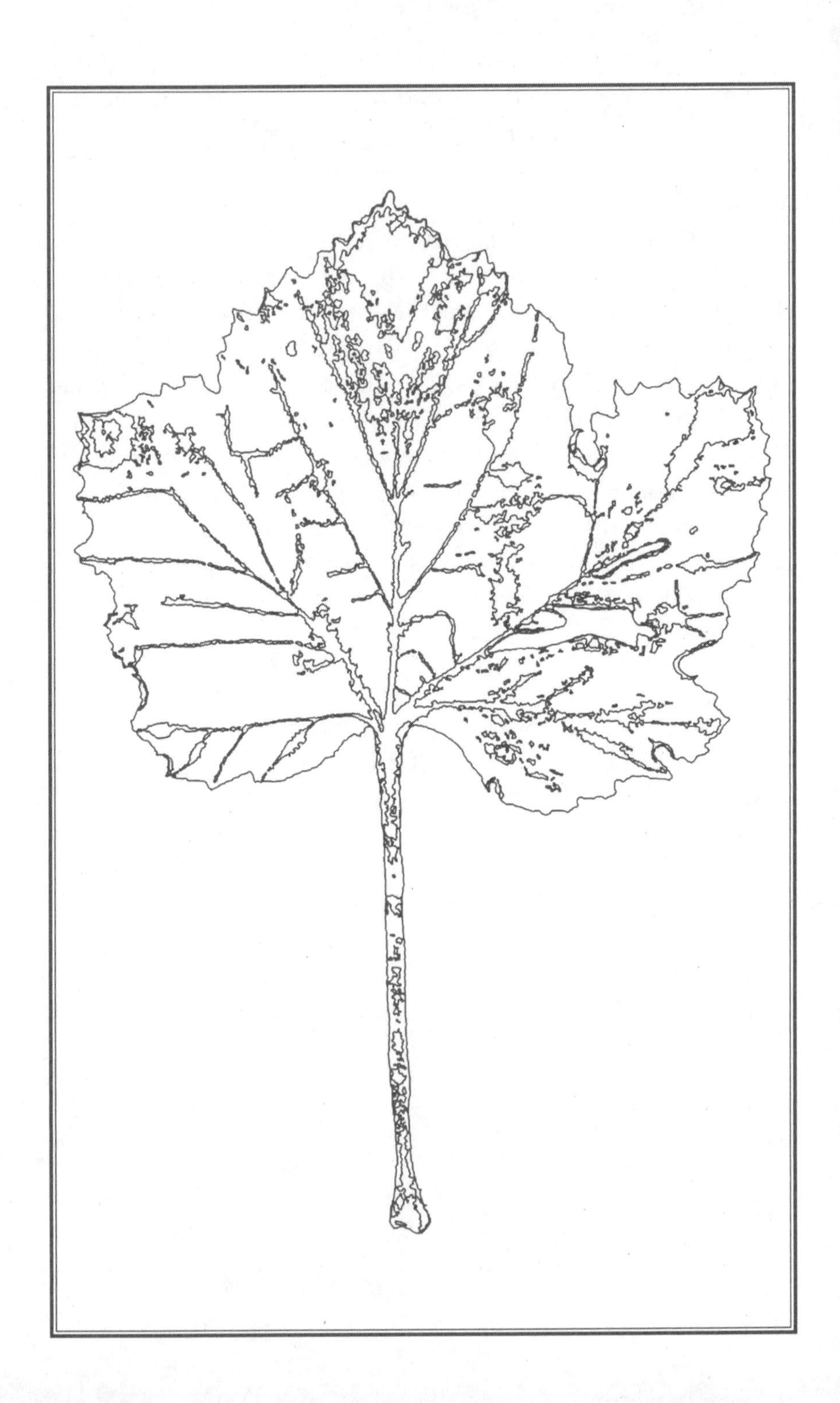

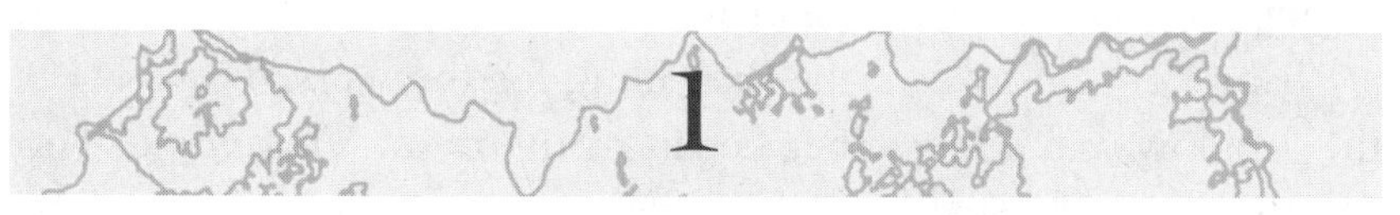

1 Season of Waiting

ADVENT

I met my friend Sam at college, back in the early seventies. Sam had been adopted as an infant in a "blind" adoption, so he grew up knowing nothing about his genetic parents. After his discharge from the Army, Sam decided to find his birth mother. It was not easy, but after some detective work, he discovered her name and the city where he was born. Nobody with that name lived in the city anymore, but by searching through phone books, he found a family with the same last name who lived in a neighboring town. He wrote them a carefully worded letter, saying he was looking for a woman—he gave her full name—who had lived in the area about thirty years ago.

A few weeks later, Sam received a phone call from his birth mother. She had heard from a cousin that someone was looking for her, and she had guessed why. She told him her name. Then she said, "Are you who I think you are?"

So they met. The reunion was cautious on both sides, and it went okay. Over coffee, Sam found out a little about the circumstances of his birth. His mother had been unmarried, and she and his father had gone their separate ways. As they talked, Sam had a sudden urge to tell her a recurring dream he had had since childhood.

In the dream, he is sitting on a bed in an upper-story room. It is not an ordinary bedroom. Instead of a door, it has a stairway that leads down into the rest of the house. From the bed, Sam can see the top of the stairs to his left. Straight ahead, he looks out a window and through a network of tree branches.

Sam went on to describe the railing for the stairs, the view out the window, and a few other details in the room. That was it. That was the whole dream.

When he finished, his birth mother gave him a strange look, then said that he had just described the room where she had stayed during the last month of her pregnancy. It was a converted attic in a boarding house in a town other than her own. She rarely left the room, finding it difficult to get up and down the stairs. She had spent that last month sitting on the bed, waiting, in the very room Sam described. After she gave birth, she never saw the room again.

This is a spooky story, but Sam is a down-to-earth kind of guy, so I believe him. In his mother's last weeks of pregnancy, she waited. It was all she could do. And that waiting, in some mysterious way, marked what she was waiting for. That time created a lasting image in her unborn child's mind.

What am I waiting for today? To be reborn myself, of course. As always. To emerge from this cocoon of impatience and doubt. To open new wings and fly. To live purposefully, with faith.

I am not the only one waiting for this miracle. When I look around me, in my home, community, country, and world, it is as if I am looking into a great mirror. My own longings are reflected back to me, my own impatience, doubts, and fears magnified to a sometimes frightening degree. At times, the world today reminds me of an egg, with its brittle shell cracking. Cracking because it is brittle, and also because there is something inside. Something alive, strong, and new, battering its way out.

If so, then we are living in a new Advent. Traditionally, in the Christian calendar, Advent is a period of inward reflection that parallels the final weeks of Mary's pregnancy. It is a time for space to open up in expectant hearts—new, empty space—ready to be filled.

Sam's story suggests that how I wait affects what is coming in ways I cannot know—and can hardly imagine. That the time of waiting does more than make space for the new thing, whatever it will be, and more than give eyes to see the new thing—though these are both great gifts. That the time of waiting is also truly a time of gestation.

In making space for the new light, I take part in its creation.

In this season of Advent,
dear God,
for the sake of new life,
let me look ahead with courage and love.
Let me act not from fear, but from faith.
And, dear God, out of my impatient nature,
may I do nothing to rush this birth,
but give it time for wholeness.
Grant me the patience to wait.
Amen.

Questions for Reflection or Discussion

Take a "waiting" approach to these questions. First, read a question over. Then, before answering it, allow one or two minutes of silence. Let the question float like a baby in the womb. At the end of the silence, jot down five to ten words that came to you during your waiting. Finally, answer or discuss the questions more fully.

- How do you prepare for change?
- Who has nurtured change in your life?
- What are you waiting for today?

Scripture Reading

Psalm 139:1–18
"Such knowledge is too wonderful for me"

O LORD, you have searched me and known me.
You know when I sit down and when I rise up;
        you discern my thoughts from far away.
You search out my path and my lying down,
        and are acquainted with all my ways.
Even before a word is on my tongue,
        O LORD, you know it completely.
You hem me in, behind and before,
        and lay your hand upon me.
Such knowledge is too wonderful for me;
        it is so high that I cannot attain it.

Where can I go from your spirit?
        Or where can I flee from your presence?
If I ascend to heaven, you are there;
        if I make my bed in Sheol, you are there.
If I take the wings of the morning
        and settle at the farthest limits of the sea,
even there your hand shall lead me,
        and your right hand shall hold me fast.
If I say, "Surely the darkness shall cover me,
        and the light around me become night,"
even the darkness is not dark to you;
        the night is as bright as the day,
        for darkness is as light to you.

For it was you who formed my inward parts;
        you knit me together in my mother's womb.
I praise you, for I am fearfully and wonderfully made.
Wonderful are your works;
        that I know very well.

My frame was not hidden from you,
when I was being made in secret,
intricately woven in the depths of the earth.
Your eyes beheld my unformed substance.
In your book were written
all the days that were formed for me,
when none of them as yet existed.
How weighty to me are your thoughts, O God!
How vast is the sum of them!
I try to count them—they are more than the sand;
I come to the end—I am still with you.

Other Suggested Scripture Readings

Psalm 130 "LORD, hear my voice!"

Luke 2:25–38 "Now there was a man in Jerusalem whose name was Simeon"

James 5:7–11 "The farmer waits for the precious crop from the earth"

A Traditional Reading for Advent

Luke 1:39–56 "My soul magnifies the LORD"

Practice

Take a walk. Wait.

Take a walk at your favorite city park, or nature trail, or beach, but don't go home as soon as you're full of the sounds and smells and the wind on your face. When you feel, "How wonderful, I have experienced the beauty of this earth, and now I am refreshed and ready to go home and make ten dozen cookies," stop. Stay. Wait. Wait until you're bored. Pass through that boredom into something new. Wait until an empty space opens up inside. Wait for new eyes to see new light, if, by grace, it comes into your life.

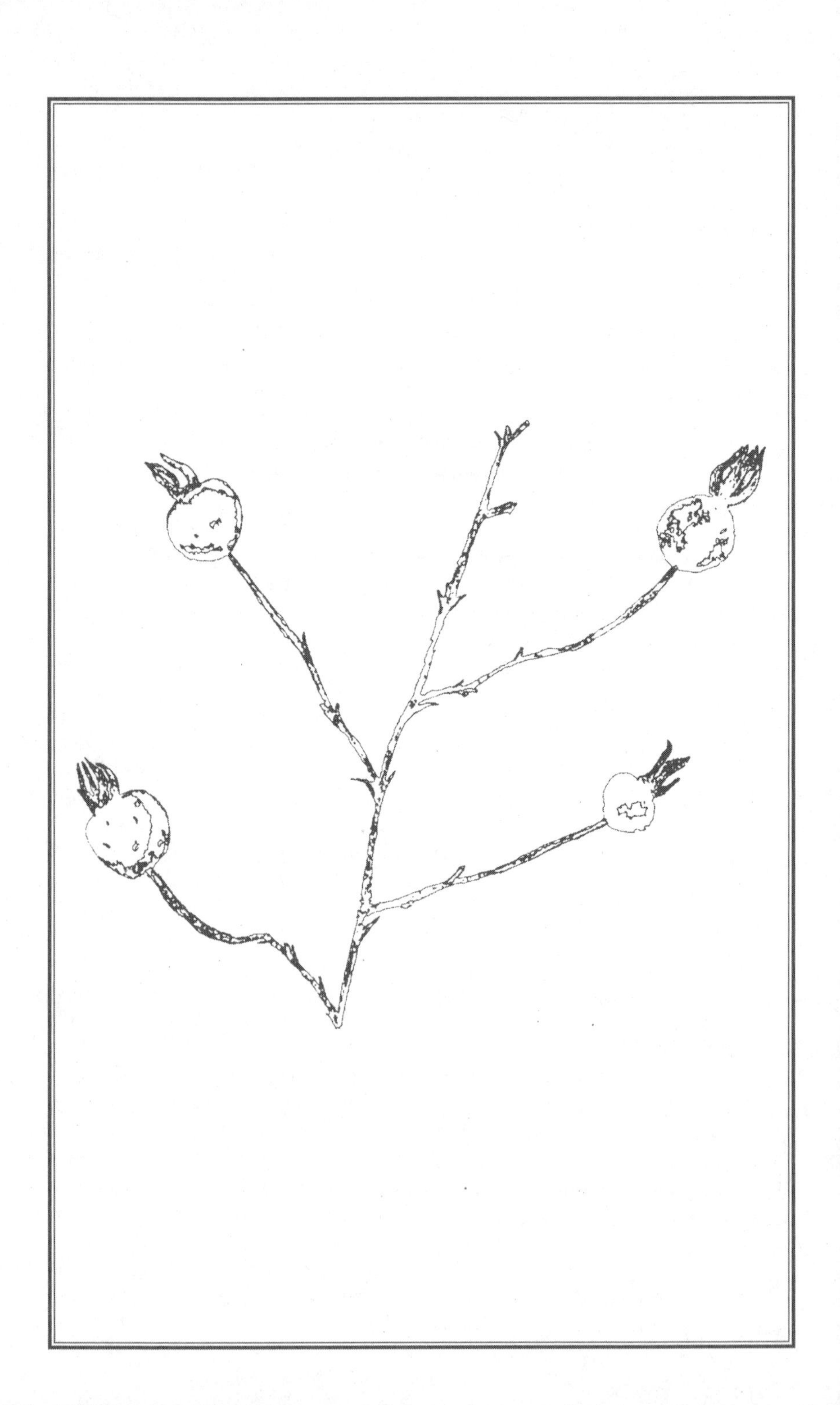

2 Leap of Faith

CHRISTMAS

My husband David's birthday falls between Christmas and New Year's Day. One year, my gift to him was conceived many months earlier, back during Lent, when I decided to add drawings to the written entries in my nature diary.

Starting to draw took a big leap of faith: I had never been good at art. I was sensitive about it and dreaded making drawings so bad that my final Lenten penitence would be repenting for ever making them.

Yet the possibilities of the written word had been shrinking around me. I would be describing something as simple as a twig or a leaf, and before I knew it, strings of adjective-laden clauses were collapsing under their own weight. Perhaps a simple drawing would say it all. Finally, screwing up my courage, I bought colored pencils and resolved to do a sketch a week for the six weeks of Lent. Forget art, I told myself. Try for accuracy. The true angle of the branch's bend. The correct size ratio between the thorn and the leaf. Draw what you see, I thought, and let God do the rest.

Before I could draw it, I had to see it. Looking closer than I ever had for writing, I noticed just how a salmonberry thorn spreads to meet the curve of the branch. How its bark up close is not really brown, but a palette of greens, grays, and pinks. This was fun, and with the fun came a new respect for the salmonberry's own self, its unique salmonberry-ness. Still, I worked fast on each drawing, hoping to leapfrog the whole talent issue and capture the heart and spirit of the subject through sheer speed.

By Palm Sunday, I had six rough little sketches. Their flaws were obvious, yet I was not disappointed or ashamed—only surprised at how irrelevant my fears turned out to be. Paging back through my Lenten nature diary, reading an entry, looking at the sketch, and seeing again in my mind's eye that particular leaf, branch, or bud on a particular day in spring—all this made me absurdly happy. In the process of drawing, I had learned a new way of looking. I liked my drawings, flaws and all, and I did not repent for making them.

Through the summer and into fall, I added small drawings to my nature diary, recording the change from bud to flower, from new leaf to old. It was not until all the leaves had fallen and the winter solstice passed that I found the nerve to make a drawing not for myself, but as a gift.

For David's birthday card that December, I drew a branch end from a Nootka rose that grows wild on our lane. Because the drawing was for him, I took special care with it, laying the branch down on the paper to mark just where the twigs came out, tracing the four fat rose hips that hung from their tips. The thorns of the wild rose, I discovered, were bigger and tougher than those of the salmonberry bush. A crown of dried sepals rested on the top of each rose hip's scarlet ball. And all along the brown twig, out of the cradles between the tough gray thorns, grew tightly packed red buds. In the spring these buds would unfurl into new leaves like toddlers taking their first steps. Now they were still wrapped in their swaddling clothes, newborn in the long, cold nights of December.

I made more nature drawings in the following months. As spring turned to summer, leaves became my subject. Summer turned to fall, the paths in the woods grew thick underfoot, and every walk offered a wealth of colors and patterns. I would pick up a leaf, bring it home, then give myself over to it, letting the drawing take all the time it took. Again and again, I would think I was finished, then see something new. Another spot, another crack, another sign of age. Another mark of this leaf's unique life—the marks that made it beautiful.

Emptying myself of expectation and trying to be true to one leaf created room in me for compassion, and then for awe. By the time each work was finished, I knew the leaf was infinitely more than any drawing I could make. My best drawing could only hint at the real thing. Still I loved my drawings, for the pleasure of making them and for themselves alone.

Throughout the aeons, millions of leaves are made by God and aged by God. For a moment of time, I had given my full and respectful attention to just one. Each leaf spoke God's word. Drawing it, I made my reply. In return, God shared with me the wonders and joy of creation.

Dear God,
I am filled with expectations,
and you are never what I expect.
By your grace may I hold my expectations
lightly, in the open palm of my hand,
for the breath of your Spirit to lift and
blow them wherever you will.
Amen.

Questions for Reflection or Discussion

- What in your life gets most of your attention?
- What brings you the most joy?
- What's the most surprising piece of your life right now?

Scripture Reading

Genesis 18:9–15
"Is anything too wonderful for the LORD?"

They said to him, "Where is your wife Sarah?"
And he said, "There, in the tent."
Then one said, "I will surely return to you in due season, and your wife Sarah shall have a son."
And Sarah was listening at the tent entrance behind him.
Now Abraham and Sarah were old, advanced in age; it had ceased to be with Sarah after the manner of women.
So Sarah laughed to herself, saying, "After I have grown old, and my husband is old, shall I have pleasure?"
The LORD said to Abraham, "Why did Sarah laugh, and say, 'Shall I indeed bear a child, now that I am old?' Is anything too wonderful for the LORD? At the set time I will return to you, in due season, and Sarah shall have a son."
But Sarah denied, saying, "I did not laugh"; for she was afraid.
He said, "Oh yes, you did laugh."

Genesis 21:1–7
"God has brought laughter for me"

The LORD dealt with Sarah as he had said, and the LORD did for Sarah as he had promised. Sarah conceived and bore Abraham a son in his old age, at the time of which God had spoken to him. Abraham gave the name Isaac to his son whom Sarah bore him. And Abraham circumcised his son Isaac when he was eight days old, as God had commanded him. Abraham was a hundred years old when his son Isaac was born to him. Now Sarah said, "God has brought laughter for me; everyone who hears will laugh with me." And she said, "Who would ever have said to Abraham that Sarah would nurse children? Yet I have borne him a son in his old age."

Other Suggested Scripture Readings

Psalm 98	"Let the floods clap their hands"
Mark 4:26–32	"The kingdom of God is as if someone would scatter seed"

A Traditional Reading for Christmas

Matthew 1:18–25	"For the child conceived in her is from the Holy Spirit"

Practice

Look at a stone.

Find a small stone or pebble and bring it to a table where you can work. The first small stone you see will probably do fine. Using words, crayons, or colored pencils, describe or draw the stone as completely as you can. The use of a less familiar tool can help you break out of predictable territory and look afresh, so if you are better with words than with drawing tools, try drawing the stone instead of using words. And if you're more comfortable drawing than writing, try writing this exercise first.

If using words, take at least ten minutes, even if you think you've said it all in five. Wait. Keep looking. A drawing will probably take longer. Give yourself permission to walk away and come back later for a fresh look, then keep working.

Resist the urge to turn this exercise into a work of art. Simply describe the stone as completely and objectively as you can.

When finished, highlight some of the final things you noticed, the aspects that did not show themselves until near the end.

If God were talking to you through this stone, what might God be saying?

3

To See with New Eyes

EPIPHANY

The largest building in the small Mexican fishing village was the church. Finished in white stucco, it sat on a rise at the end of a dirt road. I walked past one-story dwellings made of bare concrete block to get to it. Chickens scratched around outdoor clay ovens in dirt yards. Pigs inspected shadows under bushes. A woman in a dark cotton dress passed me on the road. Looking surprised, she said, *"Buenas dias."* Only a few blocks from the beachfront restaurants and bungalows where the tourists congregate, I had entered a world where a *gringa* was an unexpected sight.

After spending my whole life nestled in the English-speaking world, I had conceived a desire for adventure in foreign lands. I felt it was time to be broadened, enlightened, by travel. So David gave me a week in Mexico for my fiftieth birthday, and here I was in the small village of Encarnatión on the Mexican coast. I had arrived the day after New Year's. I spent the mornings and afternoons strolling and basking on the town's glorious beach, the evenings chatting with my fellow English-speaking pilgrims in the shared guest *cocina* (kitchen). Unlike me, they were seasoned travelers. They had visited Mexico many times, knew all the big resorts, and had returned to Encarnatión for its pristine beach and small-town character. Like a chorus, they lamented lost paradises. Acapulco, ruined. Cancún, ruined. Even

Zihuatanejo, they told me, once a placid fishing village like Encarnatión, now had taco stands, massage parlors, and T-shirts for sale, up and down the beach. How they hoped it would not happen here! Encarnatión was such a gift. One man wanted to give something back to the village in return for the peace and renewal he had found here, but he could not think what it might be.

The perfect gift, I thought, in light of their fears, would be for all of us to fly home, tell no one we had been there, and never return. But I did not say that. I wanted to come back myself someday. With a friend.

This morning, I decided to walk up to the village church. Beyond its picket fence, the road disintegrated into rock and brush. I passed through the gate into a dirt courtyard planted with ferns, snake plants, hibiscus bushes, and flowering trees. The church stood tall and white at the end of a brick path. On this weekday, the place was deserted. Yellow butterflies fluttered among the flowers. I walked the path and climbed red masonry steps to open arched doors. Just inside the church, a broken, empty eggshell lay on the concrete floor, as if a stolen egg had been eaten there by a furtive dog. The big room was furnished with hewn benches, axe strokes plainly visible in the wood. Behind the altar hung the crucifix: an emaciated Christ with greenish-gray skin and painted blood seeping from his feet, knees, side, shoulders, palms, and brow. A life-size brown Madonna stood in the corner, hands folded.

After a while I went back outside. It was the day before Epiphany, the celebration of the coming of the Magi that ends the Christmas season in the Christian calendar. Beside the brick path, an outdoor crèche huddled beneath a rough structure made of curved branches and palm fronds. A paint-spattered wooden chair sat in front of it. I sat down, offered a prayer of thanks for the continuing Incarnation, then looked over the scene. Mary and Joseph, attractive painted figures two feet tall, knelt with their backs to me. Though they looked like pieces from a set, nothing else in the crèche matched them. The animals were a hodgepodge of little worn-out toys: a couple of sheep, a plastic cow, a reindeer with glitter glued to its antlers, and two rabbits that looked like Easter bunnies. At the back of the crèche lay a bundle of white embroidered cloth with a pink plastic baby fist sticking out from the folds.

A woman and a young girl came through the courtyard gate. I said, *"Buenas dias,"* and the woman introduced herself—Kahreen, it sounded like. I pointed to myself and said, "Margarita." The girl had a string of rosary beads wrapped around her wrist. The woman said something, and I replied with one of my few Spanish phrases: *"Lo siento, no comprendo"* ("I'm sorry, I don't understand"). She smiled and shrugged. They tended to the crèche, straightening the toy animals. When they opened the swaddling clothes, the baby Jesus appeared as a Caucasian doll with the head broken off from the body. An odd and disturbing sight, but apparently no surprise to Kahreen. She clucked to herself, his body in one hand, his head in the other. I wondered if she was embarrassed for me to see their broken Jesus.

As I watched, a vision dawned inside me. I saw myself back home buying a brown-skinned baby Jesus from the cathedral store. I would mail it to the village with a note, explaining that I had seen they needed a baby Jesus, and this was my thank-offering for the use of their beautiful beach. Maybe I could find someone who knew Spanish to help me write the note.

I am not often struck by generosity, and my vision flooded me with warmth. I had come from afar, like the Magi, traveling to this remote village, hoping to be changed. Here was a welcome change—the advent of charity! This paradise had been a great and unexpected gift, and I would make my gift in return.

Then I looked again at the crèche. Where on earth did they get this weird collection of cast-off toys? In the next moments, while Kahreen and the girl talked softly to each other, and I sat peacefully dumb, the nativity scene slowly shifted in front of me, moving closer in one sense, and in another, falling away. Clearly, the toy animals and broken doll had been accumulated, piece by piece, from the parish itself. From those same concrete-block dwellings I had passed to get here. The painted figures of Mary and Joseph were the exception.

With new eyes I studied them, wondering how they came to be here. Were they the parish's first purchases of a set that they planned to complete, one figure at a time? I did not know enough Spanish to ask.

Kahreen arranged the swaddling clothes so that only the doll's head was visible. He looked okay. In a slow and painful seep, the warmth of my vision drained away. After all, the Magi had not brought Jesus with them, or sent him back from home, postage paid. They came to *find* the Savior.

The crèche belonged to the people who were born in this village, not to me. How seductive the role of generous *patrona*! But at this time and place, the best I could do, the only gift I could make, was to let those who made and loved the crèche keep it as their own. This Sunday, if I wanted to give, I could put some *pesos* in the collection plate for the parish to do with as they chose.

Straining to remember the Spanish for "church" and "beautiful," I said to Kahreen, *"Gracias. La iglesia es muy bonita."* She smiled and nodded.

I walked out of the courtyard gate, past the homes of the village, and back to the beach.

Dear God,
in choosing what to do in this world,
I need you close by me, as close as possible.
Especially when I see a place to do some good.
Let me stop a moment, turn my attention
away from myself, listen for your voice,
and look where you are pointing.
Amen.

Questions for Reflection or Discussion

- When you see someone with a problem, what's your typical response?
- When you have a problem, what do you want from others?
- How does love respond to trouble?

Scripture Reading

Psalm 36:5–9
"In your light we see light"

Your steadfast love, O LORD, extends to the heavens,
your faithfulness to the clouds.
Your righteousness is like the mighty mountains,
your judgments are like the great deep;
you save humans and animals alike, O LORD.

How precious is your steadfast love, O God!
All people may take refuge in the shadow of your wings.
They feast on the abundance of your house,
and you give them drink from the river of your delights.
For with you is the fountain of life;
in your light we see light.

Other Suggested Scripture Readings

Genesis 45:1–8a "It was not you who sent me here, but God"

Luke 10:25–37 "And who is my neighbor?"

1 Peter 1:22–23 "You have been born anew"

A Traditional Reading for Epiphany

Matthew 2:1–15 "Where is the child who has been born king of the Jews?"

Practice

Find God in a "To-Do" list.

Do you use a "To-Do" list? This practice involves paying attention to the items on your list in a new way. You might use this practice as a brief morning devotion.

First thing in the morning, take a moment to review your plans for the day. Then spend time quietly in the presence of God. Visit each item on your list, asking in turn, "Where is God in this task?" You may find answers from your own deepest values. In each task, even the most mundane, look for a reflection of what you hold sacred.

Next, ask God to meet you in the course of each activity. It's not always easy to discern what God would have you do, or how God would have you do it. What you can know is that whatever you do, God will be there.

Carry on with the day, treating the items on your "To-Do" list as seems best. At the end of the day, take a moment to review the list. How did God meet you on the way?

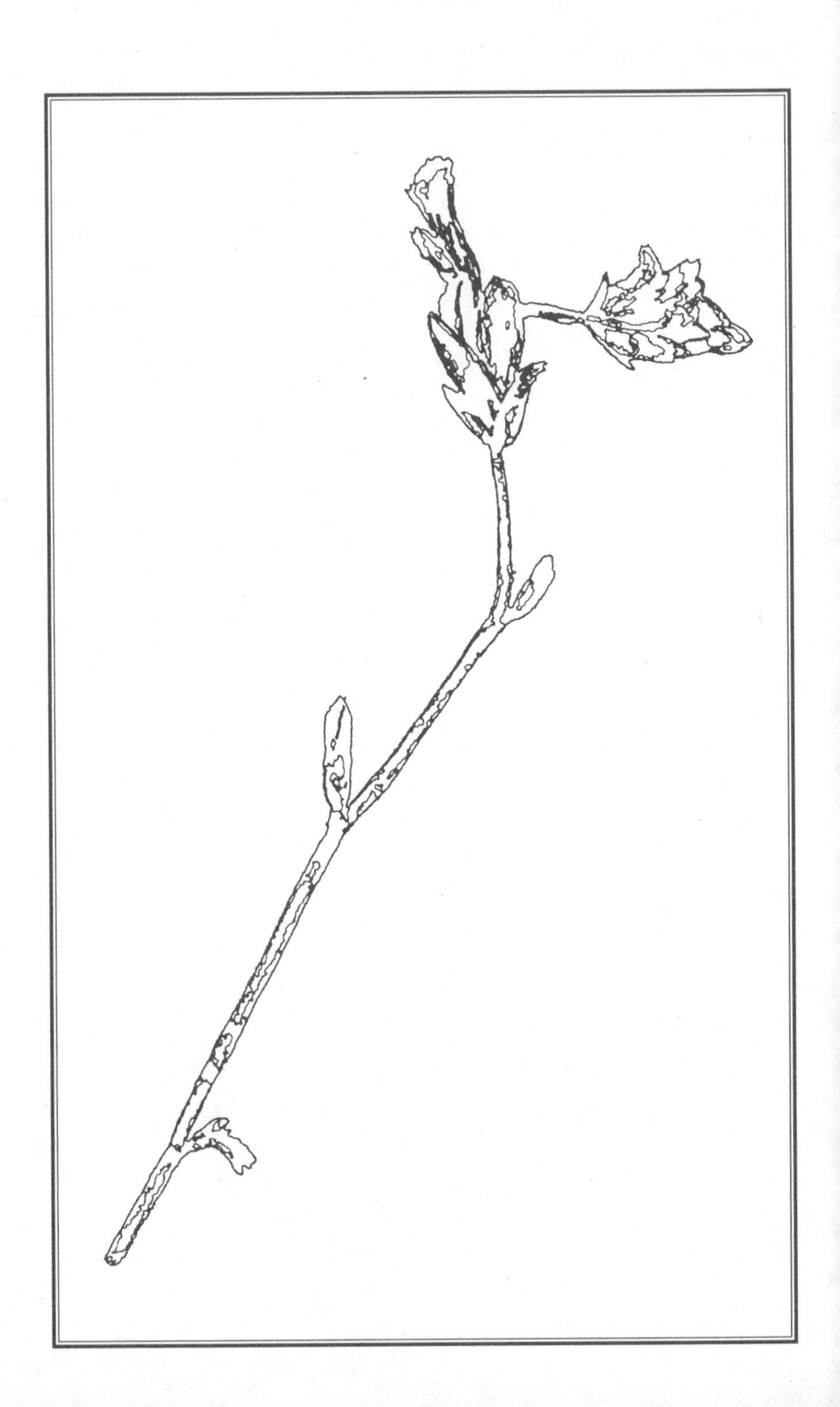

4 Hearty Fish Soup

LENT

"Hearty Fish Soup" has a solid Christian ring to it, so when it came my turn to fix soup for the Wednesday-night Lenten suppers at church, this was the recipe I chose. I chopped and sautéed onion and celery, crushed and stirred in garlic cloves, added two big cans of diced tomatoes, sprinkled in parsley and thyme, twisted a grind or two of black pepper, added a splash of white wine, and *voilà*: the base was ready to simmer.

Next, the fish—slicing and counter-slicing half-frozen orange roughy, spooning cubes of fish into the pot. When the soup was bubbling and the fish flaky, I tasted. Mmmmm. Sure hit. Better take along a few copies of the recipe for the inevitable requests.

With the pleased sense of bearing the golden egg, I placed my soup pot in a nest of potholders on the sedan's back seat and took off. After parking next to the church, I climbed out, circled the car, opened the door, and lifted out the pot of hot soup. Then I stepped back onto sloping wet grass, slipped—oh!—scrambled—no!—slipped again—eek!—and realized I was going all the way down.

For the next few seconds, I lived life to the fullest. Besides trying not to get parboiled, I also devoted myself to saving that soup. If I could keep the soup pot horizontal throughout my descent to earth, I did not care how else I came down or landed.

Couldn't do it. By the time I stopped moving, the soup stopped moving, and the ground stopped moving, I had witnessed more than half my hearty fish soup—onion, celery, garlic, tomato, parsley, thyme, black pepper, white wine, and orange roughy—erupt from the pot and land in the gutter.

On the plus side, not a drop touched me.

I picked myself up. Resisting the urge to scoop up all available soup from the gutter and pour it back into the pot, I carried the remains into the parish hall, left my three-quarters-empty pot on the stove next to two full soup pots that others had brought, and went to Evensong.

The church was warm. People smiled at me. I started to feel better. While singing the first hymn, I slowly became aware of all the voices around me. It was as if I had been given new ears—ears that could catch each voice in our small congregation, hear its unique beauty, then hear its part in the whole. By the last note, I felt much better. I had made soup, brought soup, spilled soup, and the world rolled serenely on, with me in it. The service flowed through me like a river.

After Evensong, we ate in the parish hall and had plenty—more than enough. I sampled all three offerings. Each and every bowl held the best soup I had ever tasted in my life. No one asked for my recipe, but then, no one got more than a mouthful of my soup. Conversation revolved around favorite hymns from childhood. I went home with an empty pot, a full soul, and the taste of God's Kingdom in my mouth.

That taste stayed with me for most of the next day. Then, hour by hour, day by day, "real life" piled its usual helpings of doubt and indecision onto my plate. Most of my indecision turned around a proposed expedition to St. Peter's Church in Seattle that Saturday. St. Peter's was holding an open walk on its full-size canvas labyrinth, and a few women from my parish wanted to go. The drive from our little town on the tip of the peninsula would take two to three hours each way, depending on bridge traffic and the ferry across Puget Sound. Did I want to join them? Carpool? Drive?

I had long wanted to walk a labyrinth and never had the chance. But this little jaunt would eat up a whole Saturday in spring. My garden called out for weeding, planting, tending. Also, the experience I wanted was a peaceful, reflective labyrinth walk, not six hours in a car with four chatting church ladies. As the weekend approached, I fussed over those dilemmas. By Friday evening, when I finally decided to join the pilgrimage, my taste of the Kingdom was pretty much gone.

Saturday dawned clear and beautiful. Throughout the trip to Seattle, I thought about everything I could be doing in my garden, if only I were not heading toward Seattle. Resentment and regret over lost garden time got topped by guilt, since my transparently half-hearted offer to drive had not convinced anyone, not even me. Nancy, a woman who already did so much volunteer parish work, ended up driving. I imagined she would have liked a restful Saturday as much as I would have, except that she deserved it more.

The labyrinth was painted on a huge piece of canvas and laid out on the floor of the church's gymnasium. Lighted votive candles encircled it. Our facilitator asked that we take off our shoes before walking the labyrinth. At the last minute, I took off my socks, too. Entering the path barefoot, I felt in shards, in a million little pieces. At first, I was very aware of the others around me, but eventually that part of my mind quieted down. Then it was just me, the circling path, the turns, and my feet on the path. When I arrived at the center, I stood still for a while, eyes closed.

After a few minutes, standing in the center of the labyrinth, a question rose up inside me:

"Dear God, what do you want from me?"

Immediately, an answer came back: "I want you to live."

"But how do I do that?"

"Live."

By the grace of God, it was enough. The weight on my shoulders lifted. The world stopped revolving around me. My garden would grow whether I was there or not. It was not my job to save Nancy from a gift she freely offered the rest of us. I thought of the words of

Jesus, when he said, "I came that they may have life, and have it abundantly." I thought of the moment when I watched my soup pour out into the gutter, and the hour of prayer, song, and satisfying food that followed. It was about as abundant an hour as I had spent in a while. In those moments, I knew how to live.

"Do you want me to spill my soup?" I asked.

"Live. I want you to live."

Dear God,
I am your humble servant,
falling to earth, spilling my soup,
alive in this world you made.
Amen.

Questions for Reflection or Discussion

- What person or experience has made the world come alive around you?
- What would a deeper relationship with God be like for you today, moment to moment?

Scripture Reading

Isaiah 29:3–16
"Shall the potter be regarded as the clay?"

The LORD said: Because these people draw near with their mouths and honor me with their lips, while their hearts are far from me, and their worship of me is a human commandment learned by rote; so I will again do amazing things with this people, shocking and amazing.

> The wisdom of their wise shall perish, and the discernment of the discerning shall be hidden. Ha! You who hide a plan too deep for the LORD, whose deeds are in the dark, and who say, "Who sees us? Who knows us?" You turn things upside down! Shall the potter be regarded as the clay? Shall the thing made say of its maker, "He did not make me"; or the thing formed say of the one who formed it, "He has no understanding"?

Other Suggested Scripture Readings

Psalm 131	"My soul is like the weaned child"
John 10:7–15	"I came that they may have life"

A Traditional Reading for Lent

Joel 2:1–2, 12–17 "Return to me with all your heart"

Practice

Look for God in spilled soup.

The longer I live, the more surprising God is. In the very heart of any surprise, including whatever leads up to and falls out of it, there is God.

After spilling my soup, I found the voices at Evensong and the flavor of the soup full of life and richness, without having to make any special effort to pay attention to them. It's not practical to plan on spilling the soup. Fortunately, life is full of surprises. This week, make a special effort to look for God in each surprise that life hands you, big and small, good and bad. Are you surprised into paying attention to an aspect of God's creation that you'd overlooked before? Does a surprise draw you deeper into life?

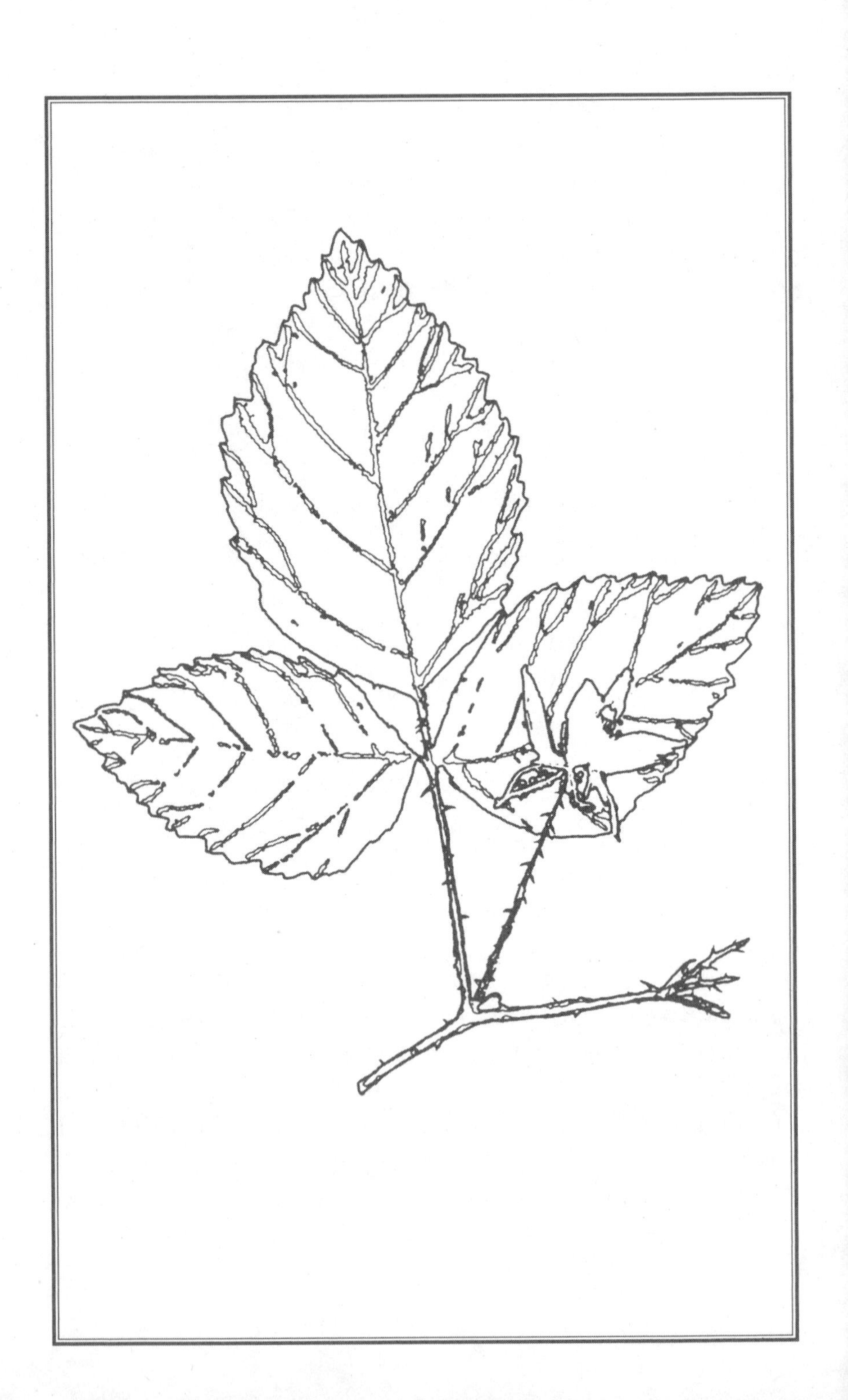

5

Just Freedom

EASTER

When my mother was a girl in the 1930s, she spent summers at her grandparents' farm near Lancaster, Ohio. The two-story farmhouse, big barn, and other outbuildings that formed the heart of Myrtle and Ira Cave's homestead were joined to a wheat field, a corn field, a hay field, and a little woods in back—all tucked into thirty acres of Ohio flatland. The farm provided most of Myrtle and Ira's sustenance, with a bit left over for sale or barter.

According to my mother, chicken had more flavor back then. "The chickens Grandmother raised and fried in her cast-iron skillet make the chickens we buy in the store today taste like almost nothing," she laments.

Myrtle and Ira Cave lived long enough to know all their great-grandchildren. I remember them both, but my mind's eye holds only a few faint sketches of their life on the farm: Myrtle's hand slipping between a roosting hen and its nest, then reemerging with two eggs cradled in her palm. The deep-throated smell in the outhouse, two dark holes for seats. A sleepover in their guest room, roses on the wallpaper, handmade quilts on the bed. That's about it.

I don't remember how the chicken tasted.

Nowadays, standing at the supermarket, looking over the packages of boneless, skinless breasts, the rows and rows of identical square thighs, I sometimes hear a powerful call from the Cave family farm, and the call feels like an echo from a world that exists outside the treadmills of time.

Myrtle raised chickens for eggs and meat. She fed her chickens on the wheat and corn that Ira harvested in his fields and then processed at the local granary.

"Grandmother had a long metal hook, like the end of a clothes hanger, only longer, that she used to catch chickens," recalls my mother. "She would pick which chicken she wanted for dinner, catch its legs in the hook, and draw it toward her. She tied the chicken up on the clothesline by its feet. Then she took her big butcher knife and whopped off its head. I had to stay away while it flopped around on the clothesline."

Once the headless chicken stopped moving, Myrtle cut it down, gutted it, and dipped it in a bucket of boiling water to loosen the feathers.

"It was my job to pull the feathers off," my mother says. "They came out really easy, a handful at a time. They smelled like wet, musty old rags."

A woodstove with a reservoir for hot water sat in a corner of the kitchen. Myrtle fed the stove with kindling that Ira brought in from the woods. After her granddaughter plucked the chicken, she burned off its pin feathers with a kitchen match. Then she cut up the chicken, dipped it in flour, and fried it in her cast-iron pan.

"What I remember best about Grandmother was her big, soft bosom. It was like resting your head on a pillow," says my mother. "I could run all over that farm. I didn't have to be afraid of anything. It was freedom."

Though I don't remember much of the farm myself, I do hold clear memories of the two who made it their home. It's true that my great-granddad Cave didn't say much. And I, too, rested my young head on my great-grandmother's big, soft bosom, a warm pillow that came with arms to hold me.

So every once in a while, instead of buying my standard big package of thighs for barbecuing, I pick out a whole chicken at the supermarket, take it home, cut it up, and use every part. Cutting up a chicken forces me to pay attention and reminds me that the chicken I eat was once a living creature, made by the same God that made me.

So how do you cut up a chicken?

I start by sharpening my knife. The knife I choose is longer than a paring knife and shorter than a butcher knife. Its blade is strong enough to break bone, but not so wide that it can't make a hairpin turn. I sharpen the knife on a whetstone that spends most of its time in the back of a drawer.

Then I place my store-bought chicken on a heavy cutting board, take hold of a leg-and-thigh combo, and wiggle it. I'm searching for the joint between the thigh and the body. The joint lies hidden under skin, flesh, and sinew. By wiggling the thigh, I can sense where the thigh bone connects to the hip bone. With my sharp knife, I slice downward between the thigh and the body, aiming for that joint. When I reach bone, I wiggle the leg around some more, fine-tuning the angle of the blade so that it fits into the socket. Then I cut through the joint and on down, separating the leg-and-thigh combo from the body.

Using the same wiggle technique, I find the joint between the leg and the thigh, then separate the two pieces by cutting through that joint. After removing the other hindquarter and both wings, I am left with the football-shaped body. I set it on end, the larger of the two cavities facing up. Then I cut down through the ribs, separating the breast from the back. Halfway there, it's easier to drop the knife and just tear the body apart with my hands.

I break the back, then cut it in two pieces. Finally, piercing the heavy breastbone with my knife and cutting lengthwise, I split the breast into two equal pieces, using brute force to break and split the bone.

That's how I cut up a chicken. Myrtle's technique was probably a little different. But it couldn't have been *too* much different, because that's how chickens are made.

Every time I cut up a chicken, I think of Great-grandmother Myrtle. It feels good to share this basic task with her across the century. Though memory is a creative companion and capable of distorting the truth, at the same time, memory has the power to draw out essence and pass it down through generations.

Real life on a farm in the 1930s was, in many ways, much harder than life is today. After all, this was the heart of the Great Depression. Myrtle and Ira worked long and hard just to feed their livestock and themselves. Even so, my mother's memories of that time focus on abundant life: ripening blackberries, just-hatched chicks, blooming flowers, sweet corn, heavenly fried chicken, and a sense of freedom that defines a place and time for her. Though the farm was enclosed on all sides by a society in a state of economic collapse, still, in my mother's memory, that sense of freedom and plenty is all that matters.

It is like Easter morning busting out of the nightmare of the crucifixion. When I read again the stories of shock and wonder that surround the Holy Week, I can't help but empathize with the Gospel and Epistle writers who first put those events into words. The details of Jesus's trial and execution would have been painful to write down, but not too hard to make believable. A young man with an unsettling message and a band of followers is arrested, tried, tortured, and killed by a ruling state. Such things happened—are happening—in the common course of current events. Everybody knows it.

But how to say what happened next? The real work would have begun when the writer turned to face the empty tomb. Writing decades after the event, stitching others' memories and faith onto their own, the Gospel and Epistle writers struggle to describe the indescribable and say the unsayable. What was the resurrection like? What does it mean? They aim to convey the truth behind their faith, knowing full well it will sound like fantasy. They teeter on a tightrope of words, using the empty cross as a balancing rod.

A grief-filled woman returns to a garden and meets a stranger there. What starts as mistaken identity turns to the shock of recognition at the sound of a well-loved voice. Everything changes, and it is all that matters.

Friends walk together sharing painful news and meet a stranger on the road who sheds new light on the recent events. What starts as a simple offer of a meal and a room for the night turns to the shock of recognition at the breaking of the bread. Again, everything changes, and it is all that matters.

At times, the stories sound to me as if these writers experienced the resurrection of Jesus Christ as a door opening into another world. A world and way of life free of the darkness and terror of death. A place where food has savor, where everyone lives safe and free. It is as if they got a glimpse of God's reality, and the door cracked open just when everyday reality was at its worst. From that angle, the life of the resurrection sounds to me a whole lot like life on the Cave family farm.

At first glance or first hearing, the old stories of family and faith might seem barely related to present life, bits and pieces from a strange and alien world, cut up and wrapped in the plastic of time.

But this is an illusion.

All I need to do is grab onto a piece, give it a wiggle, and pay attention. The joints and sinews reveal their underlying truth: that the leg bone is connected to the thigh bone, and the thigh bone is connected to the hip bone.

I cannot get to the historic Cave family farm today, not by car or by foot. Neither can I stand in the footprints of those early followers of Jesus. Still, a place of safety and freedom lives on, and that place is as real as a young girl running all over a small farm in Ohio.

Dear God,
in the midst of grief and passion,
speak my name, and I will know your voice.
Open every gate, spring every trap,
and set me free in your own world.
Amen.

Questions for Reflection or Discussion

- Describe a place where you've felt safe and free.
- How did that place and its freedom affect the rest of your life?
- What do you do now that connects you to freedom-giving events from the past?

Scripture Reading

Ezekiel 37:1–14
"Mortal, can these bones live?"

The hand of the LORD came upon me, and he brought me out by the spirit of the LORD and set me down in the middle of a valley; it was full of bones. He led me all around them; there were very many lying in the valley, and they were very dry. He said to me, "Mortal, can these bones live?"

I answered, "O LORD God, you know."

Then he said to me, "Prophesy to these bones, and say to them: O dry bones, hear the word of the LORD.

Thus says the LORD God to these bones: I will cause breath to enter you, and you shall live. I will lay sinews on you, and will cause flesh to come upon you, and cover you with skin, and put breath in you, and you shall live; and you shall know that I am the LORD."

So I prophesied as I had been commanded; and as I prophesied, suddenly there was a noise, a rattling, and the bones came together, bone to its bone. I looked, and there were sinews on them, and flesh had come upon them, and skin had covered them; but there was no breath in them.

Then he said to me, "Prophesy to the breath, prophesy, mortal, and say to the breath: Thus says the LORD God: Come from the four winds, O breath, and breathe upon these slain, that they may live."

I prophesied as he commanded me, and the breath came into them, and they lived, and stood on their feet, a vast multitude.

Then he said to me, "Mortal, these bones are the whole house of Israel. They say, 'Our bones are dried up, and our hope is lost; we are cut off completely.' Therefore prophesy, and say to them, 'Thus says the LORD God: I am going to open your graves, and bring you up from your graves, O my people; and I will bring you back to the land of Israel. And you shall know that I am the LORD, when I open your graves, and bring you up from your graves, O my people. I will put my spirit within you, and you shall live, and I will place you on your own soil; then you shall know that I, the LORD, have spoken and will act, says the LORD.'"

Other Suggested Scripture Reading

John 1:1–18 "The light shines in the darkness"

Two Traditional Readings for Easter

John 20:11–18 "Woman, why are you weeping?"

Luke 24:13–35 "Two of them were going to a village called Emmaus"

Practice

Share a visit to freedom.

This week, make a date with a friend, letting your friend know that you'd like to share stories about the experience of freedom in your lives. When you get together, ask your friend to tell you a personal story of freedom or release from fear, deprivation, or self-doubt. Listen and ask questions. Pay attention.

Then tell your friend about your own time or place of freedom.

How are your stories different from each other? What do they hold in common?

6

When the Still, Small Voice Starts Yelling

PENTECOST

It was a small problem—trivial, really. Small, personal, aesthetic—and characteristically Episcopal.

It started the Tuesday in Holy Week—the last week of Lent, between Palm Sunday and Easter. I was to serve the cup for Communion at the evening service. In my bedroom, I had put on basic black pants and a dark red top, crimson being the appropriate liturgical color for Holy Week. In the Episcopal church, lay servers often wear an alb—a white robe vestment—over their street clothes to serve the wine. But vesting is not a requirement at my parish, St. Paul's, and I liked the idea of offering the cup to my fellow parishioners as "one of them," dressed like any member of the congregation.

Wearing the liturgical colors of the season was not required either, but over the years since joining the Episcopal church, I had grown attached to this symbolism. I liked how the cloths that hung over the pulpit and lectern, and the vestments for the priest and altar, changed to support the themes of each season—from Advent's quiet blue to Christmas's gold and white; from the somber violet of penitential Lent to Holy Week's blood-red; from the black of Good Friday to brilliant gold and white for Easter and the weeks of the Easter season.

So even though I wore my own clothes to serve the wine, I tried to blend in—or at least not clash with the current seasonal palette.

My dark red top would be fine for a Holy Week service. None of this was a problem.

The problem was the cross. I slipped my cross pendant over my head, then stood in front of the mirror and stared into the reflection, frowning. The cross itself was made of green stones embedded in silvery metal. Between its four posts, Celtic knots curved and turned, filling the empty space and giving the pendant an oval shape. I like the design for its feeling of wholeness, and I also like its saintly association—the catalog had sold it as "St. Margaret's Cross."

Of all the St. Margarets (and there are a number of them), my favorite is Margaret the Virgin. By legend, Margaret the Virgin experienced an astonishing variety of miracles during a vigorous defense of her faith and virginity. At one point, it is said that she got swallowed by Satan in the shape of a dragon, then was vomited up when the cross she carried proved too irritating for the dragon's digestive tract. Beheaded in the year 304, she is the patron saint of pregnant women, childbirth, dying people, exiles, and kidney disease. If my cross were St. Margaret the Virgin's symbol, then I was happy to wear it.

But not during Holy Week. Against my dark red top, the green stones in the cross appeared positively garish, even Christmassy in an off-kilter sort of way. For this week leading up to Jesus's death, the pendant's ornate design simply felt wrong.

I sighed and took it off. That night, I borrowed one of the plain cross pendants hanging in the church sacristy and wore it for the service. I blended in, felt part of the team and part of the congregation. Problem solved.

The next time I served the cup, we were into the weeks of Easter season. The dark red top went to the back of the closet, and St. Margaret's cross came out of retirement. But the issue of the cross kept niggling at me. A vague outline formed in my mind of a pendant cross for Lent and Holy Week—plain, spare, maybe even a little rough looking. Nothing in the catalogs I had around the house matched that outline, and a cursory online search did not produce anything, either. Finally, I put it aside. After all, Lent would not come around again for months. Maybe something would turn up.

Easter season passed, and Pentecost Sunday ushered in "Ordinary Time," the longest season in the liturgical calendar. St. Margaret's cross was perfect for Ordinary Time and its liturgical color of green. The problems of Lent and Holy Week faded into the distance.

Then one June day not long after Pentecost Sunday, I sat struggling with my current piece of writing, stuck in one of those awkward places where I had to dig down and pull sentences out one by one, their roots gripping the compost pile in my mind as stubbornly as the roots that anchored the myriad dandelions outside my window. In the middle of these struggles, suddenly, a completely new and unbidden idea popped up and opened its leaves. Into my mind's eye came an image of the handcrafted garden furniture I had seen in the local nurseries, made by bending and weaving together the supple green branches of native willow trees. I did not need to buy a penitential cross—I could make one! Lots of willows grew in the woods around our house. I could braid three green willow twigs together for the vertical post. Then I would work another twig into the braid for the cross post. The green wood would cure and dry in place, creating a stable construction, like the garden furniture in the nurseries.

I am not particularly handy, but this task seemed within my grasp. And, in stark contrast to the usual distractions desperately tossed up when I get stuck in an awkward place in my work—laundry, e-mail, weeding dandelions, and so on—it actually sounded like fun.

At that point, the Disciplined Writer voice cleared her throat. "Yes," she said, "that does sound like fun. In fact, it sounds like the perfect reward for completing the first draft. Just finish the chapter, and then you can make the cross."

Okay, then. Back to squeezing out those sentences. At times, they flow like water. At other times, they stick like mud, usually because I have not yet really figured out whatever it is I am trying to say.

And sometimes it is just hell. This was hell.

While I twisted and turned, practically tying my leg to the chair so that I would not get up for yet another cup of tea, setting up yet another trip to the bathroom, questions and answers about making the cross called across my mental landscape, back and forth, loud and clear, the answers to my questions coming in a voice at once livelier and a lot more helpful than that stodgy old Disciplined Writer.

Q: How could I hold the twigs taut while braiding, so the braid would be really tight?
A: You need a horizontal dowel about the size of a pencil to wrap one of the twigs around. The two ends of that twig make two of your three strands. Keep those two strands taut by tugging against the dowel, and braid in another twig as the third strand.
Q: Okay, that might work. But once this cross is finished, how will I hang it around my neck?
A: No problem! Remember the loop formed in step one? Thread the chain—or maybe a leather cord?—through that loop.
Q: Cool. But what about this horizontal dowel? I don't see anything like that in here.
A: Easy! Just drill a hole in one of the shelves of your art table, stick a pencil in there, and you're good to go. You'll just have to find the drill.
Q: Umm … I think it's in the utility room.

Now the Disciplined Writer again cleared her throat, temporarily suspending this seductive back-and-forth. "Look," she said, "let's finish the chapter first, okay? Then we'll make the cross. It'll be fun. But 'finish your homework first, then you can go out to play.' 'Eat vegetables first, then you can have dessert.' So come on, let's dig into those Brussels sprouts!"

While my chapter lay like a dead thing on the computer screen, problems and solutions for making the cross presented themselves to me one after another, like slices of cake offered up to the guests at a wedding. The steps grew more clear in my mind. I started to see the order of things and realized that I probably would not be able to keep that order straight when I got to actually making the cross.

At this point, the Disciplined Writer offered up a compromise. "Okay," she said, "tell you what. Write down the steps. Get them out of your mind. Then go back to the chapter, finish this draft, and we'll make the cross. It will be really, really fun!"

With relief, I turned away from the computer, picked up a pencil, and jotted down the steps, so I would not forget them. Then I turned back to the chapter.

And came up against a concrete wall as high and wide as the sky. I sat perfectly frozen, unable to write a word.

Time passed. It was no use. And so it was, at last, pride and will utterly beaten to the ground, the Disciplined Writer surrendered, broken and penitent, crying out to the heavens, "Yes! Yes! All right then! Bring on dessert! Make the %?#!★ cross!"

And I did. For the horizontal dowel, it turned out an old watercolor brush worked better than a pencil. Green willow twigs did not work at all, but split and broke in my fingers again and again, so I walked back into the woods and found some wild honeysuckle vine, which held up fine. An oceanspray twig made the crossbar. Also known as ironwood, oceanspray is a local native shrub with branches as hard as tree wood. I used green garden wire to bind off the top and bottom of the braid, then crisscrossed a bit of wire around the oceanspray twig to keep the cross at right angles.

Then I sat for maybe twenty minutes, a half hour, just turning this amazing object over and over in my hands, staring with wonder and delight at my very own penitential cross.

Then I sat down to write. The wall came tumbling down, a fresh breeze blew across the land, sentences spilled out, and, within an hour, I finished the chapter I had wrestled with for days.

Dear God,
I need not only ears to hear your voice,
but also faith to follow it down the path
to where joy and energy fall like rain—
the path where all the garden grows.
Amen.

Questions for Reflection or Discussion

- What activity brings you new energy?
- How are duty, responsibility, and joy related (or unrelated) in your life?
- When and how does the spirit of God speak to you?

Scripture Reading

1 Samuel 3:1–10
"Then the LORD called, 'Samuel! Samuel!'"

Now the boy Samuel was ministering to the LORD under Eli. The word of the LORD was rare in those days; visions were not widespread. At that time Eli, whose eyesight had begun to grow dim so that he could not see, was lying down in his room; the lamp of God had not yet gone out, and Samuel was lying down in the temple of the Lord, where the ark of God was.

Then the LORD called, "Samuel! Samuel!" and he said, "Here I am!" and ran to Eli, and said, "Here I am, for you called me."

But he said, "I did not call; lie down again." So he went and lay down.

The LORD called again, "Samuel!" Samuel got up and went to Eli, and said, "Here I am, for you called me."

But he said, "I did not call, my son; lie down again."

Now Samuel did not yet know the LORD, and the word of the LORD had not yet been revealed to him.

The LORD called Samuel again, a third time. And he got up and went to Eli, and said, "Here I am, for you called me."

Then Eli perceived that the LORD was calling the boy. Therefore Eli said to Samuel, "Go, lie down; and if he

> calls you, you shall say, 'Speak, LORD, for your servant is listening.'"
> So Samuel went and lay down in his place. Now the LORD came and stood there, calling as before, "Samuel! Samuel!"
> And Samuel said, "Speak, for your servant is listening."

Other Suggested Scripture Readings

Jeremiah 1:4–9	"Before I formed you in the womb I knew you"
Acts 9:1–19	"Saul, Saul, why do you persecute me?"
Romans 5:1–5	"And hope does not disappoint us"

A Traditional Reading for Pentecost

Joel 2:28–32	"I will pour out my spirit"

Practice

Take the scenic shortcut.

Think of one activity that brings you joy. Now think of one worthy and pressing task you want to get done today, or this week. Will the sky fall if you do what gives you joy first? If not, then just this once, go out and play before doing your homework. At the end of the day, see where you are.

7

Where Possibilities Burn Bright

ORDINARY TIME

From the moment he breathed air, my nephew Rory tested and explored the full reach of his physical abilities.

On the day of his birth, he grabbed his father's finger and pulled himself to a firm, upright, seated position.

Almost as soon as he learned to crawl, Rory wanted to climb stairs. He conquered the household staircase in a single afternoon, then spent hours scrambling up and down, up and down, delighted with his new toy.

At seven months, he stood without assistance, and two months later he took his first steps.

Before forming his first complete sentence, Rory thrilled and terrified my sister-in-law by climbing the tall hemlock in their backyard. She caught sight of him just as he reached the top, perched on slender branches that swayed under his weight. Holding her voice as steady as possible, she asked her three-year-old to please return to earth. He cheerfully obeyed, moving from branch to branch with will and body acting as one.

Watching Rory grow up made me think of the words of the psalmist who calls on "sea monsters and all deeps, fire and hail, snow and frost, stormy wind" to praise God (Psalm 148:7–8). If sea monsters and stormy winds can offer praise without conscious intent, then so can human beings. It seemed to me that Rory's every new exploit made an instinctive prayer out of bone, muscle, and blood. Just seeing him move made me glad to be alive and human. When I picture three-year-old Rory perched at the top of the hemlock tree, he looks to me for all the world like a great *Alleluia!*

One summer afternoon a few years after the tree-climbing episode, my husband, David, and I joined my brother's family for a casual softball game at a local park. Early in the game, David hit a pitch and the ball took off. Before any of the rest of the fielders had moved, seven-year-old Rory took off after it. With one glance he had sensed the ball's trajectory and was in line to intersect the arc. If only his legs were longer, he might have caught it. Instead, Rory fell down, and the ball dropped to earth twenty yards beyond his reach.

"I quit!" Rory yelled, scrambling to his feet. He threw his little-boy mitt onto the grass and stomped over to the sidelines. He plopped himself on a bench, folded his arms, and set his jaw.

"Come on and play," called his mother.

"No! I quit!"

At Rory's age, I had never dreamed of catching a fly ball. My prayers at those moments were begging God, "Please send the ball far, far to the opposite side of the field." And I never grew into the coordination it takes to be an effective player on any sports team. In contrast, Rory actually had talent as an athlete—obvious talent. So I was glad when his father managed to talk him back into our softball game on that summer afternoon. Only by staying in the game could Rory work out the bond between his will and his body, when they no longer automatically acted as one.

Throughout his childhood, Rory was welcomed onto any sports team he chose to join. He often knew where the ball was going before anyone else, and he competed with an intensity that was thrilling to watch.

I remember going to one of his games and greeting my nephew on the sidelines before the opening whistle. "Hi, Rory!" I said. As far as I could tell, he did not recognize me. Once he was suited up and ready to play, nothing outside the game existed for Rory, not even friendly aunts. Neither coach nor parents had to tell him to focus this way—he just did. He was about ten years old.

In Rory's early teens, the other kids finally started to catch up with him, and he got the chance to play with teammates and opponents who could give him game. He learned how to slow down and pass the ball. How to lose, and how to learn from losing. He never stopped testing his own physical potential, and he never lost the knack of seeing what might be possible, if only he were a little quicker, a little stronger. He never stopped being frustrated by the gap between his vision and his abilities.

Then in high school, Rory made a surprising choice. He opted out of the elite youth soccer leagues, the statewide organizations with paid coaches, grueling practices, and game schedules designed to hone young athletes into future dream teams. Instead, he tried out for the high school track team. What made his choice surprising—to me, at least—was that, to start out with, Rory was not all that great at track. Sophomore year, on his best days, Rory ran in the middle of the pack.

Over the summer between sophomore and junior year, Rory attended cross-country camp, learned new training techniques, and paid attention to the way they affected his performance. When the cross-country season began in the fall, I asked Rory, "Why track?" He told me that he liked competing with himself. At track meets, he still got the thrilling intensity and adrenaline rush of competition, only now he was running against the clock, trying to beat his own personal best time in each event.

Seen from that angle, Rory's choice made perfect sense. He had always been driven by his inner vision of what was possible, not anyone else's. It always had been Rory himself that he wanted to beat. In choosing track, he just carried on with his given work, building a grown-up relationship with the energies and forces that helped to create him, and that lived inside him.

As the weeks passed, Rory's times shortened, tick by tick. As he got faster, he moved up in the pack. By spring, he was racing to win.

All summer between junior and senior year, Rory cross-trained to improve his overall fitness. In September, the track team voted him co-captain, and he seemed poised to lead his team to a successful season. Then before the fall season had hardly begun, Rory's relentless push of his body's capabilities found a breaking point: he sustained a stress fracture in his right foot. Sidelined for weeks, he began physical therapy and continued to cross-train in the early mornings before school, waiting for the foot to heal.

Though Rory returned to competitive running in the spring, his injury continued to give him problems. He was fast and placed well in his best events—just not as well, I imagined, as he had hoped before the injury. He told me that during a race, the adrenaline rush masked all other feeling. After each meet, he took ice baths to control the swelling and pain. He stuck with it, though, racing at every meet until his team was eliminated during post-season tournament play.

Growing up, I always thought the good athletes had it easy. Those jocks could not possibly know pain and humiliation like the rest of us did, those of us who got hit on the head by more volleyballs than we ever returned across a net. Now, after years watching Rory work to balance his gifts of body and spirit, watching him forced to slow down and lose, when speed and winning were what he longed for, watching him race, then ice down his foot, train, and race again, the weight of such gifts has come home to me.

I also see how much Rory and I have in common. Not on the athletic field, God knows, but in the arena where we each come to terms with our own talents.

Here I sit at my desk, hoping to wrap up this chapter today, to punch through and cross the finish line in a blaze of glory. I can see the finish line, too, just at the bottom of this page. Only a paragraph or two to go. It feels as though I ought to be able to fly from here to there, if only I try a little harder, run a little faster.

And yet, if I have learned anything about writing, then this is the precise moment to take a deep breath and let any thought of the finish line go. Slow down, pay attention. Listen. Give the words a chance to say whatever it is they are trying to say. Just stick with this sentence, and then the next. The more I think "Done at last!" the greater the odds I will trip and fall. I know—I have fallen before.

In scripture, the mysterious power of God on earth—the Spirit of God—appears in a variety of forms: as a breath, for the breath of life; as a whirlwind, to evoke overwhelming power; as a dove, for reconciliation and peace. And as flames of fire. Those flames have the power to warm the cold-hearted. Encourage the fearful. They can wake the dead and drive them out of the tomb. Those flames burn the brightest, I believe, on the very edge of human possibility, when we take off and explore the full reach of our hopes and vision.

And so today, sitting at my desk, struggling to find words, frustrated that I cannot just *will* myself to where I want to go, I think of Rory climbing the hemlock tree, branch by branch, and I pray.

O Holy Spirit of God,
open my ears to your words in my heart,
open my eyes to your world
of limitless possibility,
and let's climb this tree together.
Amen.

Questions for Reflection or Discussion

- Where do your talents lie? (If that question is hard to answer, ask friends where they think your talents lie.)
- Who in a younger generation do you see as a reflection of yourself? In an older generation?
- What is possible for you?

Scripture Reading

Ecclesiastes 9:7–11
"Go, eat your bread with enjoyment"

Go, eat your bread with enjoyment, and drink your wine with a merry heart; for God has long ago approved what you do. Let your garments always be white; do not let oil be lacking on your head. Enjoy life with the [one] whom you love, all the days of your vain life that are given you under the sun, because that is your portion in life and in your toil at which you toil under the sun. Whatever your hand finds to do, do with your might; for there is no work or thought or knowledge or wisdom in Sheol, to which you are going.

Again I saw that under the sun the race is not to the swift, nor the battle to the strong, nor bread to the wise, nor riches to the intelligent, nor favor to the skillful; but time and chance happen to them all.

Other Suggested Scripture Readings

Psalm 148 "Young men and women alike, old and young together!"

Matthew 5:13–16 "You are the light of the world"

Practice

Visit paths of possibility.

Life involves choice. How you spend most of your time—your job, your primary relationships—means choosing one possibility over another. At times, you might feel forced to turn away from an enticing possibility when a strong call or obligation takes you along another path. Or, when you were a child, you might have been drawn to some activity that turned out to be harder than expected, and you hadn't yet developed the patience to stick with it.

This week, take time to remember the possibilities that once drew you in, but that, for one reason or another, you chose not to pursue. Maybe you wanted to play a musical instrument. Maybe you have a friend or relative whom you've lost touch with and you'd like to renew the acquaintance. Spend time in memory with these paths not taken. Does one call more strongly to you today? Is it more possible now than it was before? Is there a step you can take on this path now?

Look at each path as a possibility, not an obligation, remembering that it stays a possibility whether you choose to take it up now or not.

8

Bees in the Blackberries

ORDINARY TIME

All my life I have been full of fear—all kinds of fear—and have used many tricks to evade it. Like my mother, I have a touch of claustrophobia and I avoid caves. Fear of heights keeps me off the upper rungs of ladders. I am afraid of being disliked, which is a bad one. Avoiding the dislike of others constricts your life much more than avoiding caves and ladders. And these are only some of my wide-ranging and ever-evolving fears.

Over the years, my most persistent and troubling fears have to do with whatever I am writing at the time. Fear that the truth of the matter will elude me. Or that I will not have the skill to make the truth plain. Those fears, when they are rolling around inside, make it difficult to write.

Late in the summer of 2002, as our world approached the one-year anniversary of 9/11, I tumbled into a looking-glass world of fear and reaction, a world filled with threats and demands as strange as the Red Queen's were to Alice.

It all started one perfect morning near the beginning of August. I woke up, put on sneakers, and walked out into the cool air in my pajamas to pick berries for breakfast. Vines of Pacific blackberry, a choice native fruit, climb the rock wall that is next to our raspberry patch. I picked a handful of blackberries and a handful of raspberries, anticipating how they would taste squashed on a toasted bagel.

Yellow jackets, a member of the wasp family, live in the woods around my house. Since I am allergic to insect bites and stings, when a yellow jacket started buzzing around, I walked away. It came after me, buzzing right up next to my ear. This can happen in the late summer when yellow jackets forage for their winter stores. The old adage, "Leave a bee alone and it'll leave you alone" does not necessarily apply to a yellow jacket in August. Especially when you are stealing her blackberries.

I broke into a run, made a dash for the house, closed the door, and started up the stairs to the kitchen with a sense of relief at my escape. I felt a little tickle under my pajama top. Just a little tickle close to the waistband, like a hair or a bit of cut grass that had been tossed up in the open breeze. I touched it, and … youch! She got me.

When stung, the trick is to act fast. In less than a minute, I had taken an antihistamine and applied ice. Though the area still swelled a bit, and stayed swollen and tender for days, it was not really much of a problem. I thought, this is the price you pay for living in the woods and picking blackberries in your pajamas.

A few weeks later, fully clothed and working out in the woods that surround my house, I felt that same hot stab of pain, this time on an ankle. Without even the courtesy of a warning buzz, another yellow jacket had crawled up under the hem of my jeans, gotten caught there, and jabbed her stinger right through my sock. I dropped my shovel and said something I will not repeat here.

In the minutes it took me to hobble along the uneven path through the woods and reach our front door, my ankle rapidly swelled. Then it just kept right on swelling, ice and antihistamine notwithstanding. I was off my feet for two days and walked with pain for another week.

It was during that week, the week after the second sting, a week when all the national news was filled with stories about the anniversary of 9/11, that I fell into the looking-glass world of fantasy fear and reaction.

Seated at the computer one afternoon, my foot up on a stool with an ice pack balanced on my ankle, I felt a little tickle right under my knee, inside my jeans. Just a *little* tickle.

Well. Occasionally, a yellow jacket does get in the house. Repeated stings are increasingly dangerous, since the allergic reaction can escalate. I was already a cripple from the last one. So I stood up and, with great care so as not to trap the yellow jacket between denim and skin, took off my pants. Nothing. Shook them out. No bee.

Relieved, I put my pants back on and went back to work.

An hour or so later—*tickle—tickle.* Probably nothing. A fold of fabric. A hair. Something I wouldn't have even noticed before my two stings. But … what if …

I spent the end of that summer and the first part of autumn feeling imaginary bees and taking off my pants. Taking off my pants very, very carefully, in fear of the imaginary bee.

I took off my pants four or five times a day. In my kitchen, office, living room, bathroom. In the stalls of public restrooms. Once behind a tree in a state park. I felt like a fool—but was I? Yellow jackets had shown themselves willing and able to sneak under my summer clothes and hurt me. I was afraid, and I had reason to be.

Here's what made me feel like Alice in Wonderland. During that same taking-off-my-pants period of my life, the weeks immediately surrounding September 11, 2002, it seemed as though my whole country was *also* reacting to bees—real and imaginary—in sometimes bizarre ways. We had orange alerts, yellow alerts, and more orange alerts. A sudden mass purchase of duct tape. Random and not-so-random searches at airports, train stations, subways, ferry terminals. All in response to things *we had not really noticed before.* Now, we felt a tickle and we jumped, taking off our pants over and over, even though we knew the bee might not even be there this time. We knew, from painful experience, that real yellow jackets, with harmful intent, were out there. We were afraid, and we had reason to be.

After my second sting, I was afraid even to go into the woods around our house. And even more afraid of a life without those beloved paths. In fact, such a life was too fearful to accept. So, using netting, elastic bands, and all my ingenuity, I spent hours designing and making a head-to-toe outfit to keep yellow jackets from crawling under my clothes. When finished, the getup was not very comfortable, and it certainly made me *look* like a fool. But it got me into the woods in September, which was worth all that folly and more.

Dear God,
I want my blackberries without bees!
I want to live without danger of attack.
But most of all, I want to be free to move
among the bees and butterflies in this real
world you created, secure in the faith
that you are always with me.
Amen.

Questions for Reflection or Discussion

- Name something that might scare others, but that you are not afraid of.
- What does fear stop you from doing?
- Name a courageous act that has happened in your presence.

Scripture Reading

Psalm 31:1–5
"For you are my refuge"

In you, O LORD, I seek refuge;
do not let me ever be put to shame;
in your righteousness deliver me.

Incline your ear to me;
 rescue me speedily.
Be a rock of refuge for me,
 a strong fortress to save me.

You are indeed my rock and my fortress;
 for your name's sake lead me and guide me,
take me out of the net that is hidden for me,
 for you are my refuge.
Into your hand I commit my spirit;
 you have redeemed me, O LORD, faithful God.

Other Suggested Scripture Readings

Exodus 3:1–14 "And Moses hid his face, for he was afraid"

Mark 5:21–43 "Who touched my clothes?"

Practice

Break bread with fear.

Because fear is no fun, it's hard to pay attention to it. I'd rather hurry those thoughts out the door. Trouble is, they just come knocking again, unrepentant and unchanged. This exercise is designed to make a safe place for fear to be transformed.

Take a moment to think about the most important relationships in your life. Can you name a particular fear of yours that limits a relationship, making the relationship less honest or whole than it could be?

Take another moment and think about the most important actions you take in life. You might group these actions together as your "calling"—the things you feel God calls you to do. Is there a particular fear that stops you from working at an appropriate level, so you don't achieve your calling as you believe you could?

Choose just one of these fears that came to mind. In your imagination, invite that fear to sit at your table and share a loaf of fresh bread. Then make it a threesome—ask God to take a seat as well. You might invite God the Creator, the One who makes, nurtures, and lives in all creation. Or you might ask Jesus, companion and brother, to sit with you and your fear.

Break and serve the bread. Don't try to argue your fear into submission or out the door. Rather, share your thoughts and hopes around the table. Then fall silent, listen, and see what happens.

9

Real Live Grizzly Bear Love

ORDINARY TIME

The taking-off-my-pants period of my life ended in a wilderness, far from home. I spent October of that year as a resident at the Dorland Mountain Arts Colony. Located on the edge of the high desert in Southern California, the colony offered privacy—I had my own little cabin—and also the chance to work off the public utility grids, closer to the natural rhythms of the earth.

But when applying for the residency, I had not quite grasped just how close to nature it was going to be. At the orientation meeting, Karen, the colony's director, and Robert, the caretaker, devoted most of their remarks to the chief hazards at Dorland.

Poison oak—abundant both within the colony and along the hiking trails that surrounded it.

Rattlesnakes—prone to curl up on the logs in the woodpile where I would be getting wood for my stove.

Wildfire—a swift-moving hazard in the parched sagebrush, especially during October, when every branch and twig was tinder-dry.

And finally:

Mountain lions—known to hunt the region. In fact, Karen and Robert told me that just last year, a woman about my age had been killed by a mountain lion while hiking in a neighboring county.

Trying to sound brave, I remarked what a thrill it would be to actually see a mountain lion in the wild.

"Oh," Karen assured me, "it *is* a thrill."

"And if you happen to see one, you're probably not in much danger," Robert added with a sly grin. "You *won't* see the cat that's stalking you."

"You'll be fine," Karen interposed quickly. "Just pay attention."

I paid attention! The next few days around the colony, I peered at the ground in front of me before each step, listening for rattles. I jumped every time my arm brushed an unfamiliar bush, then made a detailed study of the bush's leaves, since I could not yet identify poison oak at a glance. At the woodpile, I scrutinized each stick and log before picking it up. All the while, I clutched in my sweaty palm the small compressed-air horn that Karen had given me. She had told me to set it off if I saw a wildfire or got attacked by a mountain lion. She seemed to think I would have the wit to actually push the button.

It was during this time, the poison-oak-rattlesnake-wildfire-mountain-lion period of my life, that I finally stopped feeling imaginary bees in my jeans. Within forty-eight hours at Dorland, the taking-off-my-pants period was over.

The surprising thing was that, inside my cabin, I wrote, productively, and with little of my usual fears about being unable to write.

Days at the colony were simple. I would eat, take walks, write, and sleep. At breakfast, I would listen to NPR news on my solar-powered radio, but otherwise the outside world was far away. That was the month of the series of sniper attacks in the Washington, D.C., area. Nearly every other day came another shooting, often in a parking lot or other public space. I was gripped by the story, but it was happening in an urban area on the other side of the country. From my little cabin among the sagebrush and live oaks, I was not afraid of snipers.

The third Friday of my residency, a little cabin crazy, I hitched a ride with Karen to the nearby town and rented a car for the weekend. I wanted to eat a dinner out, catch a movie, and go to church on Sunday. Be with people. Saturday afternoon I went to a matinee at a multiplex in a big, open-air mall. Ready to see most anything, I ended up glued to my seat watching *Red Dragon*. In that movie, the hero, Will Graham, hunts down a terrifying psychopathic serial killer. He is both aided and impeded by the creepy and brilliant Hannibal Lecter, who eats the people he kills.

As the plot thickened, it dawned on me that a well-done suspense thriller might not have been my best entertainment choice, considering I would be sleeping that night alone with not much of a lock on my door. But the story caught and held me, and I thought, *Oh well.* I leaned back into my padded rocking-chair seat and enjoyed the show.

The movie let out around dusk. Scared out of my wits, I walked around the mall's sidewalks, trying to calm down enough to drive back to the colony and eventually be able to go to sleep. I passed little shops, cafes, a grocery. Mothers with kids, pushing strollers. A man in a gray suit with a good-size paunch, walking along, eating an ice cream cone.

A white pickup pulled into a space, the passenger door opened, and a girl wearing a formal blue dress and a white corsage stepped out. A boy emerged from the driver's side, dressed all in black except for his skinny, wine-colored tie. They walked across the parking lot to a restaurant where more girls in formal gowns and boys in black with skinny dark ties sat around a big, open-air table.

I wondered what the occasion might be. Homecoming at the local high school? The young people looked so beautiful, so vulnerable. Like angels. They offered up to all the image of new love.

It was then that I started to be afraid of a sniper. Not that the unknown D.C. snipers would fly across the country and choose this particular mall for their next attack. Rather, afraid because the idea had been released. It was in the air for anyone to pick up, maybe someone nearby. I knew the idea was out there, because it was in me. I felt alone, far from home, and afraid.

In one scene in *Red Dragon,* Hannibal Lecter tells the hero that his fear, Will's fear, is part of his gift. He is drenched in fear because he has an unusual degree of empathy toward the bad guys. His imagination shows him, vividly, what the bad guy might be doing or planning. Seeing the possibilities is what makes him good at his job, helps him catch the bad guy. And it fills him with fear. But he is not a coward, since he acts through and with his fear. In the end, his fear is closely joined to what saves him.

I'm especially drawn to the Gospel stories that show Jesus facing his fears. Fear is part of our animal nature, which is part of our human nature. And Jesus was human. For me, Jesus is always most compelling when he is most human.

After his baptism, at the very start of his ministry, Jesus hears a voice from heaven: "You are my Son, the Beloved; with you I am well pleased." Immediately, the Spirit drives him into the wilderness, to be tested by the wiliest inquisitor of them all. Was Jesus afraid? Even with that voice, those words to take along, how could anyone not be afraid? Near the end of his ministry, in danger, his friends also in danger, Jesus says, "Now, my soul is troubled." What is fear, but a soul in trouble?

That night, I walked around the mall troubled, thinking about fear, about the sniper, and feeling like a target. I felt terror at the evil the world contains. Felt how that evil is around us, and within us, along with all the rest that makes up our humanity. At the same time, moving through that community space, surrounded by angels, I had a moment of grace. Felt how I was part of the world, moving through it with all the people, each of us carrying whatever courage and love we could hold. In that moment, I had a sense of belonging in this universe. I felt loved. Loved along with everyone around me, snipers and victims alike. Not a soft love. Not a teddy-bear love. This was more like real live grizzly bear love, appropriate for humans—such dangerous, vulnerable, and beautiful creatures of God.

Even in my moment of grace, I felt the physical effects of fear—the heightened pulse, the shortened breath. At the same time, I felt great. And I slept that night.

Fear has been called a mind-killer. With the mind shut down, fear is free to generate the kind of anger that breaks communion and runs toward violence. And in response to violence, fear can drive us into an airtight room, where, trying to be safe, we condemn ourselves and our children to smaller lives than we might have had, if only we were not so afraid.

But that is not the only path with fear. If Jesus was afraid, that is not the path he took.

The most common command in the scripture is "Do not be afraid." All my life I have tried, I have prayed, to evade my fears, only to realize at last that I cannot escape human nature, at least not in this life. So, for me, it is important to hear the command not as reproach—"What? Afraid again? Shake it off, you weenie!"—but as courage-giving companionship. I like to think it is repeated so often because God knows I need to hear it more often than anything else.

Today, I pray for the courage that lives with love. The courage to smile and wave good-bye as the kids take off for their homecoming. The courage to cross a parking lot, my arm around my sweetheart's back. The courage to tell the truth, then live in community with the consequences, remembering that we are each made in love, and out of love.

Dear God,
grant me the courage not to run from fear,
but to walk with you. When I'm afraid,
help me to think creatively and act for a life
worth living, and a world worth living in.
Amen.

Questions for Reflection or Discussion

- In whose company do you feel unafraid?
- Name an old fear—a fear you had at one time but don't anymore. What changed?

Scripture Reading

Ephesians 3:14–21
"As you are being rooted and grounded in love"

For this reason I bow my knees before the Father, from whom every family in heaven and on earth takes its name. I pray that, according to the riches of his glory, he may grant that you may be strengthened in your inner being with power through his Spirit, and that Christ may dwell in your hearts through faith, as you are being rooted and grounded in love. I pray that you may have the power to comprehend, with all the saints, what is the breadth and length and height and depth, and to know the love of Christ that surpasses knowledge, so that you may be filled with all the fullness of God.
Now to him who by the power at work within us is able to accomplish abundantly far more than all we can ask or imagine … be glory … forever and ever.

Other Suggested Scripture Readings

Mark 1:9–13	"And the Spirit immediately drove him out into the wilderness"
Genesis 1:1–2:2	"God saw everything that he had made, and indeed, it was very good"
Ezekiel 1:28–2:9	"O mortal, stand up on your feet, and I will speak with you"

Practice

See the thorn, see the rose.

Two varieties of wild rose grow near my house: the Nootka rose and the baldhip rose. The Nootka grows in tall, thick, brambly patches along the lane, while the baldhip, half the height of the Nootka, grows in single individuals back among the trees. The Nootka's showy pink flowers are larger than the baldhip's, and as summer turns to fall and winter, the Nootka's large globular scarlet hips provide a splash of color against tangles of bare branches, while the smaller baldhip nearly disappears into the forest.

Still, I have a special fondness for the baldhip rose. Its flowers may be smaller than those of the Nootka, but they are also more brilliantly colored, from pure pink to deep scarlet. Also, I can recognize the baldhip rose at any time of year just from its prickles. Each and every one of its branches and stems, from trunk to twig, is thickly armed in straight, sharp needles. Summer, fall, or winter, it's impossible to pick a single rose or hip from this bush without getting pricked.

When dealing with a situation or task that makes you fearful this week, pay attention first to what's scary about it, then look closely for something beautiful that might be joined to it in any way. Initially you might want to say nothing's beautiful about the situation. Hold that judgment in check. Take your time, and keep looking until you see something, however slight, with beauty or positive meaning. Take a moment to describe each aspect of the situation—both the scary part and the beautiful part—out loud or in your journal.

The idea behind this exercise is not to end up thinking, "Oh, that beautiful thing made it all worthwhile! The fear was worth it!" Maybe the fear wasn't worth it. The idea is to look closely enough to see all that the situation contains. Make the effort to note both the nature of the prickles and the nature of the rose.

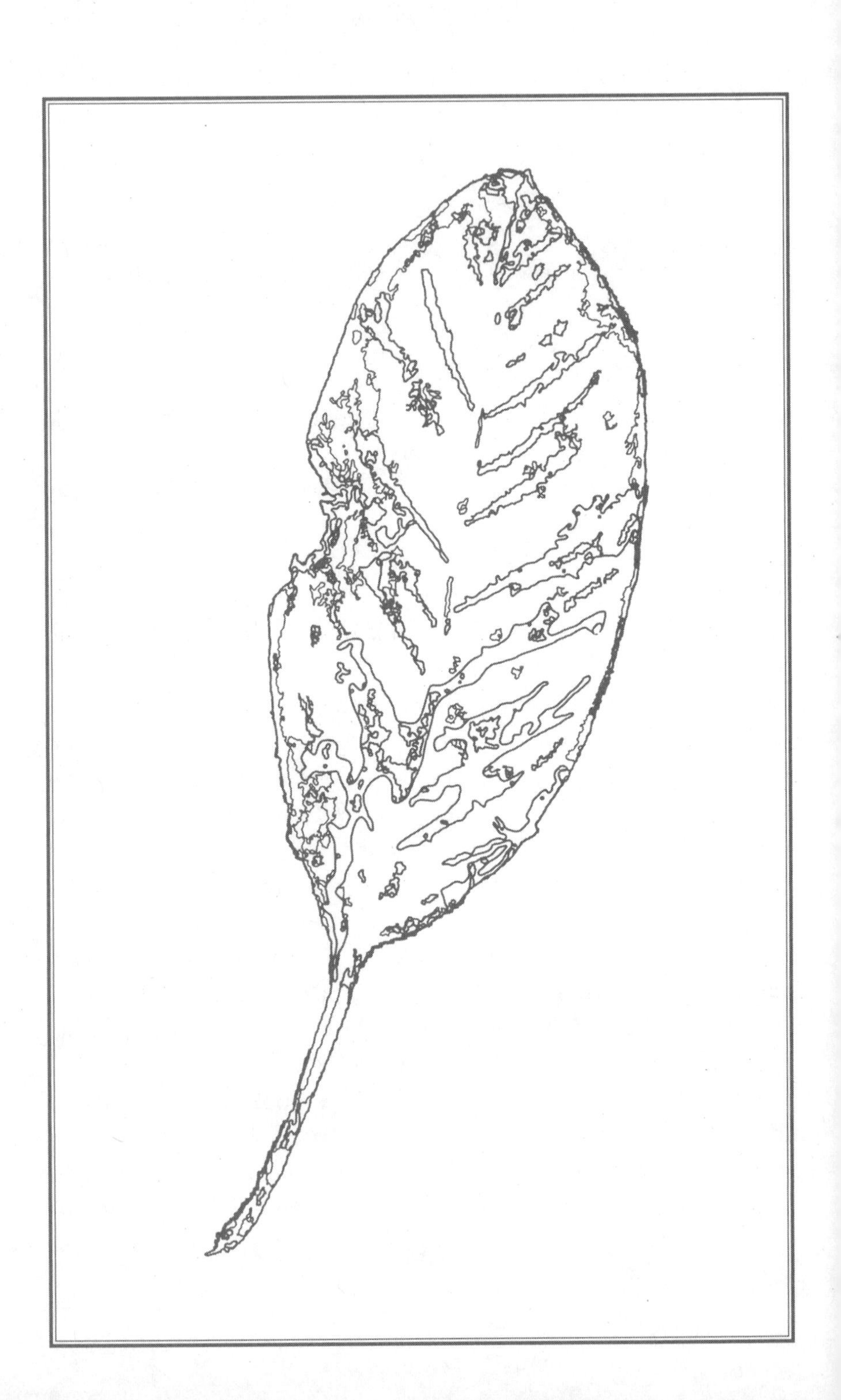

10

Lectio Divina Meets Haiku

ORDINARY TIME

I ran my eyes down the list of lectors for the coming month, and my own name popped out at me. Hurray! I had completed the training and received my license. Now for the first time I was scheduled to read two passages of scripture out loud during a service. Snatching my Bible off the shelf, I checked for my assigned passage, hoping for a really juicy text. Maybe the prophet Isaiah, promising salvation to the people of Israel? Or the apostle Paul on the nature of love? What fun to shape the sounds of those great sentences, let their meaning rise up and rap the congregation on the head.

Hmmm. Second chapter of Genesis, verses 18 through 22. Are we still in Creation? I flipped open the Bible, found the page, and—oh, no! Don't tell me I have to read those words as if I mean them!

In this section of the Creation story, having already made a man and a garden for him to live in, God decides that the man needs "a helper as his partner." First, God tries to solve the problem by creating a variety of animals and birds. The man gives each new creature its name, and yet, somehow, neither cows nor sparrows fill the bill as his partner. Finally, God causes the man to fall asleep, takes a rib, and creates a woman out of it. Hey, presto—the little helpmate! Problem solved!

Yes, indeed. And then Eve gets to deal with this male fantasy for the next five thousand years.

Somehow when I took the lay reader training, I had not anticipated standing in front of my home congregation and reading aloud words that made me feel uncomfortable, or words that I would not know what to think of, or—worst of all—words that I considered untrue. Couldn't I please read from the first chapter of Genesis instead, the other version of the Creation story, the one in which man and woman are created together in the image of God? Please?

Sorry, no. That's the way it is with the lectionary. You don't get to choose 'em; you just get to read 'em. So that afternoon in my office, I scanned the passage, groaned, and started to read the verses aloud.

It was good writing, I had to admit. The sentences rolled off my tongue. Especially near the end, when the man speaks after seeing the woman for the first time:

"This at last is bone of my bones and flesh of my flesh."

As I said those words, the image of my husband's hand sprang to mind. I saw it clearly—I know David's hand almost as well as my own—and felt it enclosing mine, his grip sure and steady. Bone of my bones, flesh of my flesh. My heart turned over.

Then Adam goes on to say, "This one shall be called Woman, for out of Man this one was taken." And the steam started sizzling under my collar again.

In short, the good stuff in Genesis's second Creation story—bone of my bone and flesh of my flesh—sits side by side with the stuff that gives me problems. Preparing to read the text aloud gave me the chance to think about it, wrestle with it, and recognize its beauty. Also, if I had not fought my way through the whole passage, I would not have had that heart-turning moment with the bone and flesh of my own life partner. That moment was worth a lot.

Years have passed since I first read the Sunday lessons at St. Paul's, and through some dozens of assignments, it has become obvious that the lectionary gods have it out for me. Again and again, I have drawn a passage that, at first glance, I would cheerfully excise from the canon. True, these passages are not rare. The Hebrew and Christian scriptures do not fit me like leotard and leggings. Still, when faced once again with reading about the vengeance of Yahweh, or the convoluted reasoning of Paul, I have to wonder, Why me, O Lord?

Then I settle down to practice, and more often than not, the answer comes back: because I have something to say to God, and God has something to say in reply. We need to talk, and this particular passage breaks the ice and lets the conversation begin.

That is one of the things church does for me—sets out a path for regular encounters with God in scripture, then provides tools to help me slow down and pay attention. And I need that help. In grade school, I was a fast reader right from the starting gun and took pride in being the fastest in my class. Whenever the teacher staged a timed reading exercise—results to be posted on the bulletin board—I always came in first and was not above cheating to maintain that rank. Growing up, I never broke the habit of tearing through reading material as fast as my eyes and brain could run. Today, with Web pages designed for scanning and clicking, and text on television screens scrolling and flashing, a well-practiced skim can seem like the only way to read.

The Bible, however, does not reveal much to skimmers. Serving as lector helped me hook into the text, because reading aloud, especially to others, takes a kind of focus that is completely foreign to the quick skim.

When my church offered a class in *lectio divina*—the ancient monastic practice of reading scripture aloud, followed by reflection, prayerful engagement, and contemplation—I hoped to learn another tool to help me along the path.

But unlike serving as lector, the practice of *lectio divina* felt awkward to me. I had trouble getting the hang of it. Not until *lectio divina* stumbled against a quite different tool for paying attention—not until *lectio divina* met haiku—did I find myself chatting along that path in a back-and-forth conversation with God.

I learned *lectio divina* in a five-week course at St. Paul's. Each Wednesday night, after a simple supper of shared soup and bread, we practiced reading scripture out loud and listening for God's voice. We paid particular attention to the language in the passage, to the words and phrases that resonated in our hearts. We shared with each other how those words and phrases spoke to us at that moment in time. It was a slow process with lots of space for silence and repeated readings of the chosen passage. Our leader, a retired Presbyterian minister, encouraged us to practice *lectio divina* at home during the week between meetings.

The idea behind *lectio divina* appealed to me. I know that words carry power, and that their power rises and falls with the tides of daily life. In the Wednesday-night meetings, I enjoyed listening to the voices of older folks who had spent a whole lot more time reading scripture than I had.

But at home during the week, practice was rough. At my desk in the morning or in bed at night, I tried to slow down, to focus on individual words and let them sink in, but I just could not keep that speed reader in check. It was frustrating—and humbling—to realize that I did not have the patience to hook into the text without the bait of a live audience to come.

Then the following winter, I took a poetry class that included a session on writing haiku. Haiku is a Japanese verse form known for distilling the essence of a moment through strong nature imagery. For the class, the teacher brought in a few objects from nature—a flower, a branch, a stone—and had us choose one, then spend time looking at it and jotting down all the descriptive words and images that came to us. From those jottings, we picked one or two words to begin writing a haiku: a single verse with three lines of five, seven, and five syllables.

It was much easier to slow down and pay attention to a stone than to a passage of scripture. Unlike my grade school teacher's reading competitions, our poetry teacher did not turn the exercise into a race. Instead, we were told to take our time. It worked. I wrote a bunch of haiku and had fun doing it.

And the next time I tried *lectio divina,* something clicked over. Suddenly, I was able to see the scripture passage the same way I saw the stone: not as a chance to win another race, but as something worth spending time on for its own sake. Reading the passage, then reading it again, I paid attention to individual words and phrases as if they were fissures and bumps in a stone. The process felt natural and true. The haiku that came in response also felt natural and true. After writing my haiku, I went back and read the scripture passage one more time. The words on the page had not changed, but my relationship to them had been transformed. I copied my haiku onto a little yellow sticky note and pressed it onto the page next to the passage.

Today, my Bible is filled with little yellow stickies, each containing its own haiku. Some draw out a theme from a verse or passage. Some argue back. Some use a word from the passage to take off in a completely different direction. Others express a realization about my own spiritual life that the passage inspired. When I leaf through my Bible, there they are, my own personal running conversations with God.

To the One who makes the path
and stands at every crossroad, I pray.
Dear God, people have always sung songs and
told stories about their encounters with you.
Can I find you in their words?
Can you find me?
Amen.

Questions for Reflection or Discussion

- When and where do you encounter scripture?
- What passages in scripture come easily to your mind? What kinds of things are you doing when you think of them?
- Prayer involves talking and listening to God. In your experience, how does the conversation start?

Scripture Reading

Ecclesiastes 3:1–8
"A time to keep silence, and a time to speak"

For everything there is a season, and a time for every matter
under heaven:
a time to be born, and a time to die;
a time to plant, and a time to pluck up what is planted;
a time to kill, and a time to heal;
a time to break down, and a time to build up;
a time to weep, and a time to laugh;
a time to mourn, and a time to dance;
a time to throw away stones, and a time to gather stones
together;
a time to embrace, and a time to refrain from embracing;
a time to seek, and a time to lose;
a time to keep, and a time to throw away;
a time to tear, and a time to sew;
a time to keep silence, and a time to speak;
a time to love, and a time to hate;
a time for war, and a time for peace.

Other Suggested Scripture Readings

Luke 4:16–30 "He unrolled the scroll and found the place"

Hebrews 4:12–13 "The word of God is living and active"

Practice

Write a prayer from scripture.

For this practice, reflect on this chapter's scripture reading from Ecclesiastes using these steps:

- Take a moment for silence, becoming aware of God's presence.
- Slowly read the passage, then read it again, listening with both heart and mind.
- Jot down a few words or phrases from the text that "rise up" and carry energy for you at this moment.
- Now put the passage aside and turn to the words you jotted down. Spend time with the memories, feelings, and associations they carry to you.
- Write a short prayer that includes at least one of those words.
- Write a haiku that includes at least one of those words. (It's okay to use a different form of the word if it works better in your prayer or haiku. For example, if the word "sew" is on your list, it's okay to use "sewing.")

To help you get started, here's the haiku response I wrote to this passage:

> God sews birthstones and
> death stones into the silver
> chain of the seasons.

Return to the scripture passage, read it one more time, then read your prayer and haiku response.

Take another moment for silence in God's presence.

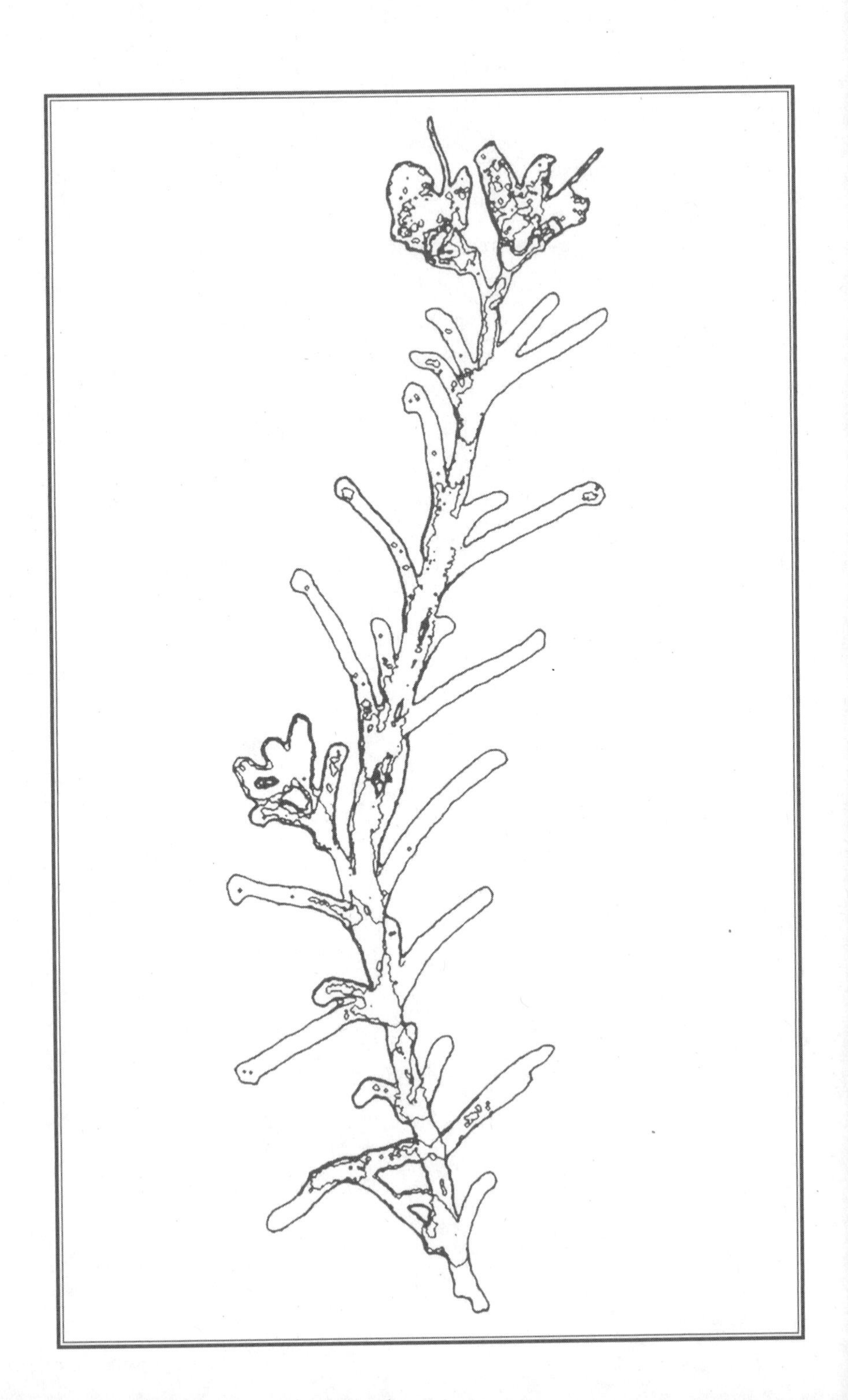

11 The Newcomer and the Old-Timers

ORDINARY TIME

Though still a newcomer at St. Paul's, I said yes when the rector asked if I would update the church history for the parish's 135th anniversary. The project suited my technical-writer background, and I expected to learn a lot about my new church community.

Along with a pile of files labeled "History, St. Paul's," Jim handed me a list of old-timers in the congregation to interview. I did not recognize any of the names. It had been less than a year since David and I had moved to Port Townsend, and most of our friends were also new to town. Before making any calls, I skimmed over the files, which included earlier histories of the parish and yellowed clippings of local newspaper articles that featured St. Paul's. If I had taken more time and paid more attention, I might have been better prepared when I called the home of Harry and Jessie Pollard, the first household on the list.

"Hello, this is Margaret McGee from St. Paul's. Is this Jessie?"

"Yes."

"Jim Phinney suggested I talk to you and Harry. I'm working on an update of the parish history, and I wonder if I could stop by sometime and talk with you about your experiences at St. Paul's."

Long pause—long enough for me to stop and realize how this call would come out of the blue to her. Here was a person she had never heard of before, introducing herself as the writer of the parish history. We had probably never even laid eyes on each other, since I attended church at ten o'clock on Sunday mornings, and most of the old-timers on the rector's list were eight-o'clockers, devoted to the early service and its more traditional language. Too late, I wished I had said "Mrs. Pollard" and "Mr. Pollard" instead of "Jessie" and "Harry."

"Did you say your name was Margaret McGee?" Jessie finally asked.

"Yes."

"Are you by any chance related to the McGee's on Franklin Street?"

"Umm ... no. I just moved to town a year ago."

"What are your parents' names?"

I swallowed. "Roger and Esther McGee. They live in Ohio."

Long pause. At last, Jessie said she would talk with her husband about it, and they might call me back. What was my phone number? When I told her, she immediately asked, "How were you lucky enough to get that 'three-eight-five' exchange?"

I understood the question. During Jessie's younger days, phone numbers in Port Townsend had consisted of only four digits. Even when the standard seven digits came in, a single exchange was plenty for the little town. Founded in 1851, Port Townsend had boomed in the 1880s as a commercial sailing port, then busted when the railroad stopped on the other side of Puget Sound, turning Seattle into the region's major transportation center. The town eked along during the Depression with the help of a paper mill, maritime trades, and a small military fort that closed down after World War II. Then in the 1980s, an influx of retirees, craftspeople, and artists brought new financial life, along with other "progress," such as a second local phone exchange and the first parking problems in one hundred years. Because we had moved to town so recently, by rights our extension should have been "three-seven-nine," marking us as newcomers. I explained that although my husband and I had moved to Port Townsend only last year, we had gotten our phone number five years ago when we had bought our property and started building.

Another long pause, during which I figured that five years of local property ownership meant less than nothing to this woman. By the time we had bought land and started building, Port Townsend's transition from military and mill town to artists' colony and tourist town was already well under way. The Pollards had lived here through that transition and for decades before. I was a rank newcomer.

Finally, she again said she would talk with her husband, and they might call back, but she didn't know when. I asked if it could be in the next few days. She didn't know. We said our good-byes and I hung up, convinced I would never hear from the Pollards again.

I was wrong. The next evening I got a call from Harry himself, a friendly, expansive call in which he said that he and Jessie would be happy to talk to me about the parish history. We set up an interview for three o'clock the following afternoon. I wondered whether Jessie had made a few calls herself and found out I really was a member of her home parish. However it happened, I was in.

The next day, Jessie, a small woman with softly curled gray hair, greeted me at the door of the Pollard home. She served tea and cookies, then the three of us sat around the massive, old dining room table. Harry's gray hair was cut short, and his dark eyes looked at me sharply from a deeply lined face. The lower part of his right arm was missing, replaced by a prosthesis that ended in a metal mechanism for a hand.

To prepare for the interview, I had read up on how to write church histories from materials provided by the diocese, and I had brought with me a list of questions crafted to start the reminiscences flowing.

"How can we help you?" asked Harry.

I read off question number one: "When did you first come to St. Paul's?"

Harry shook his head. "No, no," he said. "That's not what we're doing. This isn't about us. Didn't you say you're writing the church history?"

"Yes, that's right. But—"

"Then ask us about St. Paul's."

Long pause, this time from me. Hadn't I just done that? I rolled his words around in my mind. The next five minutes were rough, while I pitched one after another of my prepared questions and Harry batted them all straight back, reminding me that the history was about St. Paul's, not about them. Jessie sat quietly sipping her tea.

Finally, I fell silent and scanned my remaining questions. Every one was designed to get the subjects to talk about themselves. Every one was apparently useless. I shuffled papers. My gaze fell on the rector's list of old-timers. Were they all going to be like these two? Tea, cookies, and a stone wall? I had been in the Pollard home for ten minutes, and we had already run out of things to say to each other. I did not want to end the interview abruptly, but I could not think of any other questions to ask.

What did Harry mean, "Ask about St. Paul's"? From my standpoint, the history of St. Paul's was sitting right in front of me. Where was it from his standpoint? In desperation, I picked out two other names out from the list of old-timers.

"So, you probably know Corolla and Russell Sheffer?" I hesitantly asked.

The names hardly left my mouth when the feeling in the room transformed. Jessie smiled. Harry beamed. "Of course! Now, those two are important to the history of St. Paul's. Corolla was on the Altar Guild with Jessie, and Russell served on the Bishop's Committee. Let me tell you about the time Russell ..."

Bingo. Once I knew enough to ask about everybody else on my list, the stories flowed.

I heard about how Russell Sheffer (and Harry) used the paper mill's equipment to put the leather-covered cushions on our kneelers. I heard about how Mrs. Mac McCleary (wife of Col. McCleary, commanding officer at the fort) ruled the roost in the Altar Guild when Jessie was a young guild member. I heard about how the men in the church (including Harry) got rid of the vicarage's old claw-foot bathtub by sliding it upside down out the second-story bathroom window. At the end of our hour, I stood and closed my notebook, extremely satisfied.

"Thank you, Mr. Pollard, and Mrs. Pollard," I said.

Harry raised his eyebrows, and as he walked me to the door he put his arm around my shoulders. "Mr. Pollard!" he exclaimed. "Now, I like the sound of that!"

"Don't you get that very often?" I asked.

"You kidding?" he said. "What I usually get is, 'Hey, you!'"

Something told me I was the one being kidded just then.

The Pollards and the other old-timers I visited painted a picture for me of a parish quite different from the St. Paul's I knew. For example, they raised their families in the parish. Total membership may have been smaller in those days, but the tables at potlucks seated more children than grandparents. Now, our pews are filled with grandparents, and on special occasions the grandkids come to visit. And yet despite all the changes, it was clear to me that the parish they remembered was still alive in St. Paul's today, the passages of its long life linked together in an unbroken chain of time and spirit. Not all the old-timers I interviewed were quite as cantankerous about talking about themselves as Harry Pollard had been. (Thank God!) Still, the subject was never themselves alone, but always communion and community, at work and in the making.

Now I sometimes think of Harry and Russell when my knees rest on our comfortable kneelers. Sometimes I think of Jessie and Mrs. Mac when I stand before the altar. When I use the vicarage bathroom, I sometimes imagine an old claw-foot tub sailing out its window.

And while applying coats of oil finish to the doors of our new Parish Hall—a big, expensive, heavy-footed newcomer to the parish—I thought of those who had lovingly maintained the old Parish Hall, now sold and moved to another property. The old-timers I interviewed had built its kitchen cabinets, renovated its bathrooms, painted its walls. For their service, they had my gratitude and respect. In putting my own time and sweat into the new hall, I hoped, in a small way, to join with them in building the future of our shared community.

Harry Pollard died eight months after our interview. Along with his time at St. Paul's, he had served many years on the local county fair board, and his memorial service filled a building at the fair grounds to overflowing. Jessie followed him two years later. Her service filled our church building to overflowing. I had not known the Pollards as well as other people knew them, but still I wanted to be there. So I went to each service and felt I belonged, not quite the newcomer I used to be.

Dear God,
we are all newcomers,
and we are all old-timers,
in a world struggling to make community.
Bring us together with ears alert to hear
your voice and eyes wide to see your face
in the holy communion of life.
Amen.

Questions for Reflection or Discussion

- When have you welcomed change?
- Who has welcomed you in?
- Right now, where are you a newcomer? Where are you an old-timer?

Scripture Reading

1 Corinthians 12:13b–21, 24–26
"One Spirit … one body"

We were all made to drink of one Spirit.
Indeed, the body does not consist of one member but of many. If the foot would say, "Because I am not a

> hand, I do not belong to the body," that would not make it any less a part of the body. And if the ear would say, "Because I am not an eye, I do not belong to the body," that would not make it any less a part of the body. If the whole body were an eye, where would the hearing be? If the whole body were hearing, where would the sense of smell be? But as it is, God arranged the members in the body, each one of them, as he chose. If all were a single member, where would the body be? As it is, there are many members, yet one body. The eye cannot say to the hand, "I have no need of you," nor again the head to the feet, "I have no need of you." ... God has so arranged the body ... [that] the members may have the same care for one another. If one member suffers, all suffer together with it; if one member is honored, all rejoice together with it.

Other Suggested Scripture Readings

1 Kings 17:8–24	"Bring me a morsel of bread in your hand"
Matthew 15:21–28	"Woman, great is your faith!"
Acts 8:26–38	"How can I, unless someone guides me?"
Micah 4:1–5	"Neither shall they learn war any more"

Practice

Listen to wisdom.

Old-timers have a wisdom that comes from being part of a community's history. Without that history, the community wouldn't exist. Without their wisdom, the community falls apart.

Newcomers bring wisdom into a community from the outside. Without that cross-pollination, the community will someday shrivel up and die.

This week, choose to spend some time with either an old-timer or a newcomer in a community that's important to you. The community could be your place of worship, your place of work, your neighborhood, or your extended family. Choose a community that matters to you, one which you are a member of yourself.

In the time you spend together, listen for the unique wisdom this person brings to the community. You might ask to hear about an experience or an idea that involves the whole community. You don't have to agree with this person's point of view, or even accept the idea. Just listen with an open heart.

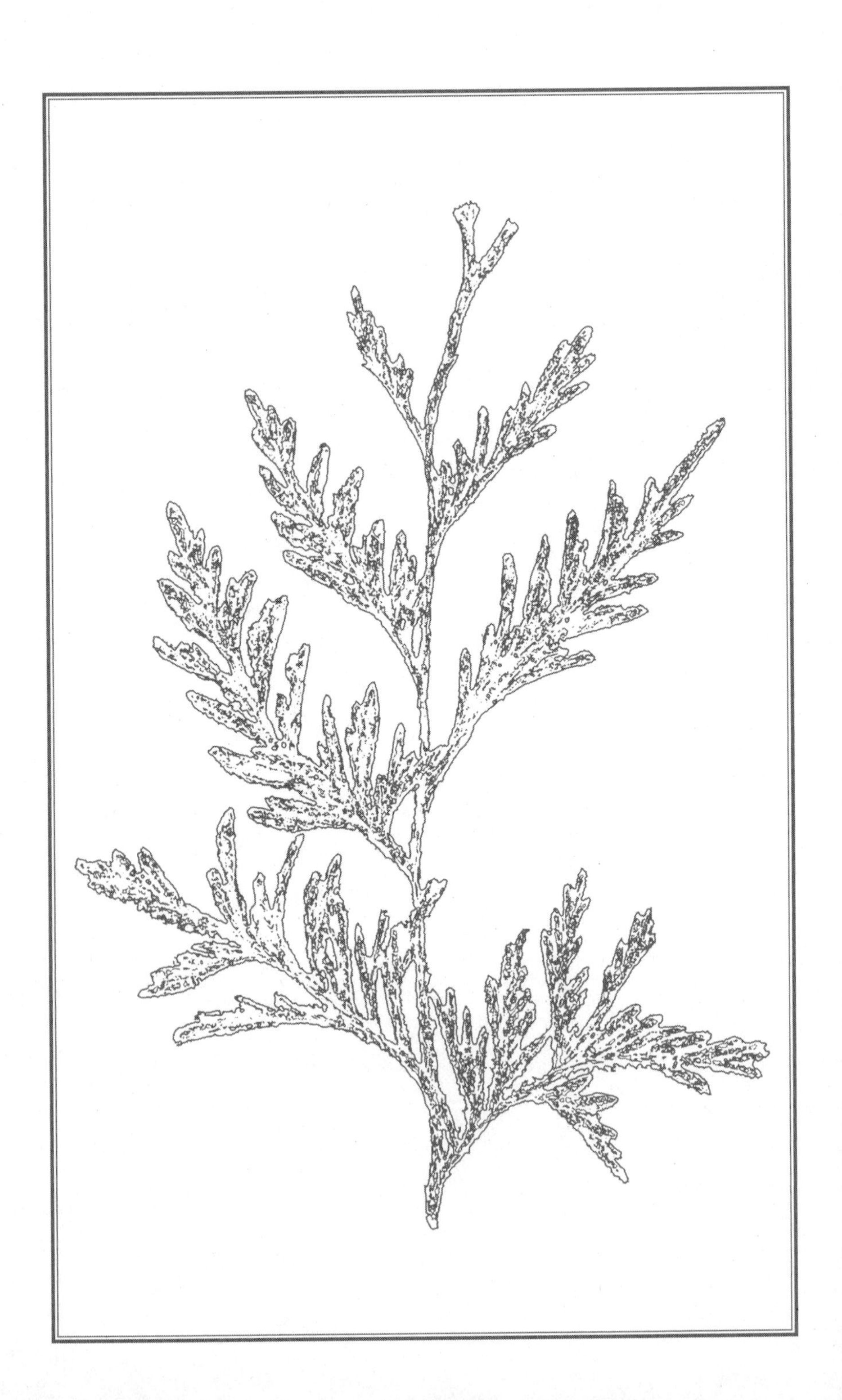

12

By Myself in a Cloud of Witnesses

ORDINARY TIME

I'm out behind the house, axe in hand, standing between a cedar stump and a pile of bucked-up fir that needs splitting before we can burn it in the metal potbelly fireplace that sits on our deck.

I set a section of fir trunk on the stump, then stand with my legs apart, the eight-inch round of wood directly in front of me. I lift the heavy axe and aim its head straight down, checking the angle that the blade will take, making sure that if I miss the section of trunk, and the blade continues down, it will hit the cedar stump, not my leg. Even if I make a glancing blow that changes the angle of the blade, it will still miss my leg. It will also miss my foot. I strike down, hit the center of the round, and it splits cleanly into two halves. I balance one of the halves on the stump and split it into two quarters, then do the same with the other half.

Four satisfying pieces of wood for the fire.

My father taught me how to split wood. He showed me how to stand and how to aim the blade so it would not hit my leg if I missed my mark. He told me not to make a big swing, but to aim straight down and let gravity do some of the work.

Before I got the hang of it, the heavy axe head often glanced off the target, tumbling the piece of wood onto the ground. I would put down the axe, pick up the wood, balance it on end again, lift the axe, aim, and freeze as my father's voice said, "Wait, wait, wait. Now, look how you're standing. Where would that axe go if the wood weren't there?" Lo and behold, if I missed my target, the axe blade would continue down toward my leg. Or ankle. Or foot.

So I would straighten up, center myself on the target, stand with my legs slightly apart, lift the axe, aim straight down, and strike. And, most likely, miss the heart of the round, pick up the piece of wood, and do it all over again.

I do not know how many times my father stopped me to point out that, once again, I had forgotten to stand so that the axe would absolutely, positively, not hit my leg when it fell. He seemed to have an obsession about this aspect of wood-splitting, and he warned me often enough so that awareness of this issue seeped into my very being.

What I did not know then, and learned only years later, was that my father's grandmother, Grace Weaver McGee, died from an axe wound. She had stayed on the farm that she and her husband worked together during his lifetime, keeping it going for another twenty years after he died. One afternoon while chopping wood, she missed her mark and cut her leg. The wound turned septic, and at the age of seventy-seven she died from illness brought on by the infection.

My father remembers his Grandmother Grace as a tall woman with penetrating blue eyes and bell-like laughter. She was known for her custard pies, crisp doughnuts, and smoked meats, which she cured over slow-burning fires made from wood that she chopped herself. At the moment of her passing, my father was in the room with her, along with other family members. He was ten years old.

Though she died before I was born, Grace is with me in spirit on this pleasant Sunday afternoon, alongside my father, reminding me to slow down and pay attention, helping me into prayer. After a few axe strokes, a safe stance becomes second nature and my father's voice fades away. I sink into the work, into a state of pleasure from the repetitive motions, from being focused and competent, and from the fresh pile of split wood.

In this state, an inner door swings open for a host of spirits to pass through. At church, I pray next to other people in the pews, and that feels good. But when I am by myself with my axe, there is no telling who might drop by—living or dead—past, present, or future—to join in my prayers, and to show the separate parts of my life as linked, one to the other, in an underlying wholeness.

I pick up a bigger round and place it on the cedar stump. This section, which comes from the base of the trunk, is too big for the axe. I find a hairline crack that extends from the center of the round out toward the bark skin, take my wedge, and line up its narrow edge with the hairline. Then I grasp the extra-heavy sledgehammer near its head and, letting gravity do most of the work, strike the blunt end of the wedge. The wedge sinks into the round of wood far enough to stand on its own. Then I step back, check my stance, and with two sharp blows—whomp! whomp!—drive the wedge down, splitting the round in two. I use the wedge again to split these two big pieces, then return to the axe, ending up with eight or ten nice-size pieces for the fire.

The air is sharp with conifer scent. In my mind's eye, I see one of the carpenters who built our house standing off to the side, his belt loaded with tools. He nods approvingly. "You can be on my team," he says. He likes it that I know how to use the right tool for each part of the job.

I pick up a round that has branch ends sticking out on three sides. As well as making knots in boards, branches also literally tie the trunk together, making it much more difficult to split. I start with the wedge. At my first sledgehammer blow, the wedge sinks cockeyed into the round, and the unbalanced round tumbles off the stump, wedge and all, and rolls away.

I retrieve it, laboriously pry out the wedge, and start again. This time, after repeated blows, the wedge gets stuck, buried all the way to its smooth crown. Using the head of my little hatchet, I pry it out and start again. It gets stuck again. The previous two pieces split so easily. I could just toss this one aside. This single piece of wood is taking longer to split than it will to burn. Could it possibly be worth the effort?

Carol, a mentor from my early days as a technical writer, stands beside me. I remember the first time she marked up one of my attempts to explain how to use a relational database. Oh, the shock of seeing my hard-wrought text eviscerated by her pencil, my precious pages bleeding red! The drudgery of incorporating all those changes! And the slow dawn of understanding as, one by one, the knotty sentences split into clear, simple prose.

I take a deep breath, laboriously pry the wedge out, and start in on the knotty piece of wood again.

Finally the round splits in two. I switch to the axe, but these pieces still won't give up with one clean blow. The axe blade sinks into one of the halves, then I lift it, wood and axe together, and pound it down, using the stump as an anvil. Pound, and pound, until finally the axe blade works its way to the bottom and the piece falls into two misshapen, knotty quarters, which I toss onto the pile of split wood.

After the second half of knot-filled fir finally yields to the axe, I choose a section with no branches sticking out for my next piece to split. There are plenty of knots in the world. No need to tackle them all at once.

I'm about done with this chore for now. I split one more round in two, then slice thin pieces of kindling from the halves. One clean stroke for each piece. I could switch to my hatchet for this job, but instead just choke up on the curved redwood handle of the axe. Though it's heavy, I don't have difficulty balancing it in my hands. It's such a good axe.

Memory takes me back to the first house that David and I lived in together, a little blue bungalow located in an urban neighborhood of Seattle. This house had a fireplace, and we found an old wedge and a sledgehammer in the basement. A classified ad in the paper led us to a cord of rounds, dry and ready to be split, a real bargain. But our dollars were stretched thin, and new axes in the hardware store costly. I bought a small hatchet instead, thinking that with the wedge and the sledgehammer, I could make do. I set up one of the big rounds near our front porch to use as a platform.

Soon, I was proudly splitting wood in full view of every window on the crowded city block. Mostly I used the wedge and the sledgehammer, since the hatchet was too small for anything but slicing up pieces of kindling. It was a laborious business, setting the wedge and lifting the heavy sledgehammer again and again. But thinking of a fire with David in our new home made the time slip by.

Out of the corner of my eye, I saw movement on the other side of the street. A neighbor, an older woman who lived alone, came down her porch steps. I did not know her name. She rarely came out of her house. The curtains on her windows were always shut tight. She walked toward me carrying an axe crossways in her arms, as if it were a child. She walked up the concrete walk to our porch.

"You can have this axe," she said, offering it to me. I took it, too surprised to reply. "It was my husband's, before he passed away," she said. "He split our wood with it. I heard you out here. You might as well have it." She turned away.

"But—but—" I sputtered, "can't I—"

"No, no." She raised a hand and let it fall, walking away from me. "You have it. It's yours now."

"Thank you!" She crossed the street. "Thank you!" She climbed her porch steps, went back into her house, and closed the door. I looked down at the axe's graceful redwood handle, its black blade. I held it in both hands, felt the balance. What a good axe.

Twenty years later, it's still a good axe. I have split enough wood for this afternoon. I put away my tools and begin stacking up my new firewood.

All afternoon, at prayer with my axe, I was never alone. My prayers were made among clouds of witnesses.

My father. Great-grandmother Grace. The carpenter who built our house. My writing mentor, Carol. David. Our neighbor in Queen Anne. Her departed husband. Each passing through the inner door from quite different worlds—or so it seems. All connected, one to the other, in this simple task.

Dear God,
let me welcome into my heart
every spirit you send to me,
and help me find some reflection of you
in all the voices of my life.
Amen.

Questions for Reflection or Discussion

- Who taught you a favorite task or pastime that you still do today?
- Where do you find wholeness, a sense of connection among the parts of life?

Scripture Reading

Matthew 10:40–42
"Whoever welcomes you welcomes me"

"Whoever welcomes you welcomes me, and whoever welcomes me welcomes the one who sent me. Whoever welcomes a prophet in the name of a prophet will receive a prophet's reward; and whoever welcomes a righteous person in the name of a righteous person will receive the reward of the righteous; and whoever gives even a cup of cold water to one of these little ones in the name of a disciple—truly I tell you, none of these will lose their reward."

Other Suggested Scripture Readings

Psalm 107:1–9	"Those he redeemed from trouble and gathered in from the lands"
Hebrews 12:1–3	"Since we are surrounded by so great a cloud of witnesses"

Practice

Split wood with knots.

It's satisfying to split a round of "clear" wood—a piece with no knots in it. A few axe strokes, and the job is done. Splitting a piece with branches sticking out on all sides is quite different. Everything slows down. But the two tasks have at least these things in common: a sharp axe, and the possibility of injury if an axe stroke falls the wrong way. Whether the wood is clear or knotty, it is important to pay attention.

Take a moment to review the typical activities of your week. Choose something that you usually do on "automatic pilot." (Brushing your teeth might be an example.) Now think of another activity that's more like splitting wood with knots—an undertaking that *can't* be done at top speed, and that requires your full attention.

At least once this week, treat each of these activities with the kind of care it takes to split wood. When you come to the activity that you normally rush through, slow down. Resist the urge to go on "automatic pilot." Instead, take care with every stroke. (For example, if you're brushing your teeth, give your full attention to each individual tooth.)

When you come to the task that requires you to slow down and give your full attention, invest your attention with the kind of care you take for your own well-being or the well-being of ones you love. Hold the idea that your attention is not only getting the job done right, but also keeping you safe and whole.

At the end of the week, write down how it felt to do each of these activities "with a sharp axe in your hand" and what changed in the way you did it.

The idea behind this practice is not to learn to live every moment as though you are swinging an axe. Rather, it's to learn to offer respect and care to each activity, whether the wood is clear or knotty.

Afterword

RETURN

Human beings are an itchy-footed species. We strike out on our own and see things our own way. This cast of mind defines our nature and our relationship to God. Even in our creation stories, we start right out by breaking the one rule the Creator gives us.

"What is this that you have done?" God asks Eve, evidently surprised that this nice new couple would actually use the gift of free will to eat forbidden fruit. Then God promptly kicks both of them out of the Garden of Eden.

It's the start of a long and difficult relationship.

Again and again in the Bible, the people and God cry out to each other, their voices filled with pain, anger, regret, and longing.

> A voice on the bare heights is heard, the plaintive weeping of Israel's children ... they have forgotten the LORD their God: Return, O faithless children, I will heal your faithlessness.
>
> JEREMIAH 3:21–22

Again and again in my life, I get caught in the surface of things. Enamored of my own goals, ensnared by endless "To-Do" lists, dazzled by self-expectations and the expectations of others, numbed by the noise and fast-cut images of the contemporary world. The daily grind grinds on. Layer by layer, a hard, dead shell of inattention cuts me off from the Reality that lives in all reality—from the living, beating heart of God. I cannot seem to stop this process. It comes from who I am and how I am made.

What I can do is return.

> The LORD protects the simple; when I was brought low, he saved me. Return, O my soul, to your rest.
>
> PSALM 116:6–7

Mysteriously, just as I am made to wander off on my own and get lost, I am also made in God's own image, as God's own child, and the road back home is built into me.

> "Return to me, and I will return to you," says the LORD of hosts. But you say, "How shall we return?"
>
> MALACHI 3:7

All I have to do is slow down and look. The world that dazzles me on its surface was made by God and is inhabited by God, right down to its core. When I take the time to stop and pay attention—to a dream, a leaf, a broken doll, a bowl of soup, a state of fear, a place of freedom, a word of scripture, a cloud of witnesses, the face across the table—then God is there waiting for me, just at hand, breaking through the hard, dead surface, calling me back to life.

> If you return, O Israel, says the LORD, if you return to me …
>
> JEREMIAH 4:1

Practicing Sacred Attention

I first wrote the stories in this book as separate pieces during a time when I was writing other things too. Because themes of *paying attention* and *prayer* seemed to rise up from these particular pieces, I started to wonder if they might go together to make a book. I told a friend about my book idea and showed her some of the drafts. After reading them, she said she liked the stories, but wasn't sure if they'd help others find God in the world around them.

"You have all these wonderful anecdotes about finding meaning in different parts of your life," my friend said, "but what about the people who say, 'I don't have a great-grandmother who chopped her own wood, or a neighbor who gave me her dead husband's axe.' What about readers who have just ordinary lives?"

I was taken aback. My stories are all about looking at leaves, making soup, listening to family histories, getting bee stings, struggling with work, going on vacation. Stuff like that. Mine is a very ordinary life.

And most of the events recorded in this book did not hold much deep meaning for me while they were actually happening, either. It is only when I start to pay attention—and pay attention to what happens when I pay attention—that connections and meaning rise up wherever I look. And I didn't start to pay real attention—sacred attention—until I began to engage with God's world, by drawing a leaf, or recording a dream, or taking the time to quietly reflect on a memory that held special energy, though I may not have yet understood why.

The following pages are for your own practice of sacred attention. You can use them to respond to the practices in this book—record a reaction to any story, prayer, or question in *Sacred Attention*—or develop your own personal practice.

If you are reading *Sacred Attention* with others, you might want to share what you put here with your group. Or, if you are reading on your own, you might set down here what you want to share with God alone. Think of these pages as a companion who's always interested in what you have to say.

Your conversation with God can begin at any moment of attention. Slow down, look, and listen. Then turn the page and make your reply.

Practicing Sacred Attention

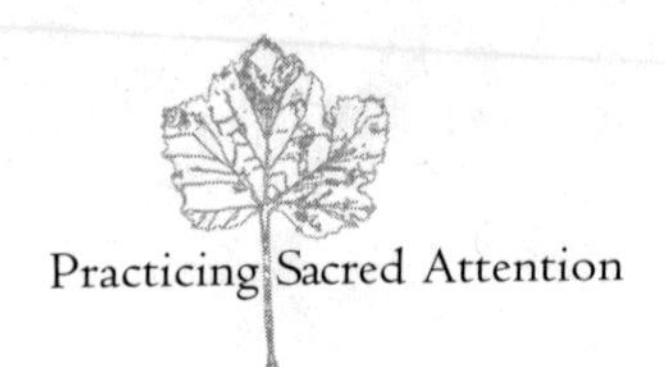

Practicing Sacred Attention

Practicing Sacred Attention

Practicing Sacred Attention

Practicing Sacred Attention

Practicing Sacred Attention

Practicing Sacred Attention

Practicing Sacred Attention

Suggestions for Further Reading

Here are a few good books for help and inspiration in the practice of sacred attention. I have included two field guides for the region where I live. Your local bookstore can recommend similar books for your locale.

Anonymous. *The Cloud of Unknowing.* Edited by William Johnston. New York: Doubleday, 1973.

Brother Lawrence. *The Practice of the Presence of God.* Boston, MA: Shambhala, 2005.

Corcoran, Nancy. *Secrets of Prayer: A Multifaith Guide to Creating Personal Prayer in Your Life.* Woodstock, VT: SkyLight Paths, 2007.

De Caussade, Jean-Pièrre. *The Joy of Full Surrender.* Translated by Hal M. Helms. Orleans, MA: Paraclete Press, 1986.

Fenelon, Francois de Salignac de La Mothe. *The Royal Way of the Cross.* Translated by Hal M. Helms. Orleans, MA: Paraclete Press, 1982.

Lionberger, John. *Renewal in the Wilderness: A Spiritual Guide to Connecting with God in the Natural World.* Woodstock, VT: SkyLight Paths, 2007.

Lyons, C. P., and Bill Merilees. *Trees, Shrubs, and Flowers to Know in Washington and British Columbia.* Vancouver, BC: Lone Pine Publishing, 1995.

Peck, Alice, ed. *Next to Godliness: Finding the Sacred in Housekeeping.* Woodstock, VT: SkyLight Paths, 2007.

Pennington, M. Basil, Thomas Keating, and Thomas E. Clarke, eds. *Finding Grace at the Center,* 3rd ed.: *The Beginning of Centering Prayer.* Woodstock, VT: SkyLight Paths, 2007.

Pojar, Jim, and Andy MacKinnon, eds. *Plants of the Pacific Northwest Coast.* Vancouver, BC: Lone Pine Publishing, 1994.

Schmidt, Gary and Susan M. Felch, eds. *Autumn: A Spiritual Biography of the Season.* Woodstock, VT: SkyLight Paths, 2005.

———. *Spring: A Spiritual Biography of the Season.* Woodstock, VT: SkyLight Paths, 2006.

———. *Summer: A Spiritual Biography of the Season.* Woodstock, VT: SkyLight Paths, 2007.

———. *Winter: A Spiritual Biography of the Season.* Woodstock, VT: SkyLight Paths, 2003.

AVAILABLE FROM BETTER BOOKSTORES. TRY YOUR BOOKSTORE FIRST.

Global Spiritual Perspectives

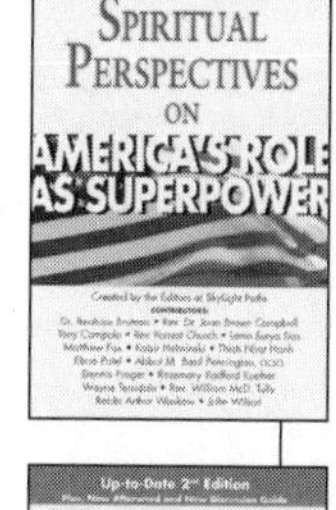

Spiritual Perspectives on America's Role as Superpower

by the Editors at SkyLight Paths

Are we the world's good neighbor or a global bully? From a spiritual perspective, what are America's responsibilities as the only remaining superpower? Contributors:

Dr. Beatrice Bruteau • Dr. Joan Brown Campbell • Tony Campolo • Rev. Forrest Church • Lama Surya Das • Matthew Fox • Kabir Helminski • Thich Nhat Hanh • Eboo Patel • Abbot M. Basil Pennington, OCSO • Dennis Prager • Rosemary Radford Ruether • Wayne Teasdale • Rev. William McD. Tully • Rabbi Arthur Waskow • John Wilson

5½ x 8½, 256 pp, Quality PB, 978-1-893361-81-2 **$16.95**

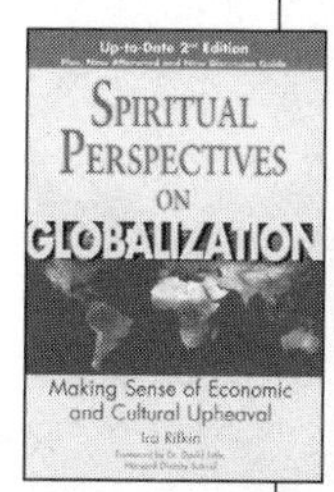

Spiritual Perspectives on Globalization, 2nd Edition

Making Sense of Economic and Cultural Upheaval

by Ira Rifkin; Foreword by Dr. David Little, Harvard Divinity School

What is globalization? Surveys the religious landscape. Includes a new Discussion Guide designed for group use.

5½ x 8½, 256 pp, Quality PB, 978-1-59473-045-0 **$16.99**

Hinduism / Vedanta

The Four Yogas

A Guide to the Spiritual Paths of Action, Devotion, Meditation and Knowledge

by Swami Adiswarananda 6 x 9, 320 pp, HC, 978-1-59473-143-3 **$29.99**

Meditation & Its Practices

A Definitive Guide to Techniques and Traditions of Meditation in Yoga and Vedanta

by Swami Adiswarananda 6 x 9, 504 pp, Quality PB, 978-1-59473-105-1 **$24.99**

The Spiritual Quest and the Way of Yoga: The Goal, the Journey and the Milestones

by Swami Adiswarananda 6 x 9, 288 pp, HC, 978-1-59473-113-6 **$29.99**

Sri Ramakrishna, the Face of Silence

by Swami Nikhilananda and Dhan Gopal Mukerji

Edited with an Introduction by Swami Adiswarananda; Foreword by Dhan Gopal Mukerji II

Classic biographies present the life and thought of Sri Ramakrishna.

6 x 9, 352 pp, HC, 978-1-59473-115-0 **$29.99**

Sri Sarada Devi, The Holy Mother

Her Teachings and Conversations

Translated with Notes by Swami Nikhilananda; Edited with an Introduction by Swami Adiswarananda

6 x 9, 288 pp, HC, 978-1-59473-070-2 **$29.99**

The Vedanta Way to Peace and Happiness *by Swami Adiswarananda*

6 x 9, 240 pp, HC, 978-1-59473-034-4 **$29.99**

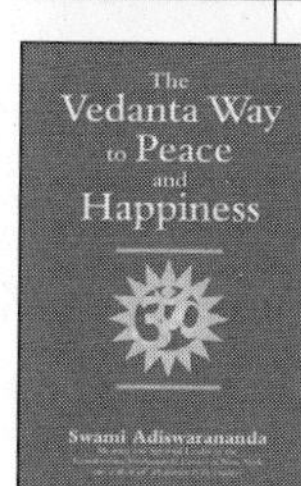

Vivekananda, World Teacher: His Teachings on the Spiritual Unity of Humankind

Edited and with an Introduction by Swami Adiswarananda

6 x 9, 272 pp, Quality PB, 978-1-59473-210-2 **$21.99**

Sikhism

The First Sikh Spiritual Master

Timeless Wisdom from the Life and Teachings of Guru Nanak *by Harish Dhillon*

Tells the story of a unique spiritual leader who showed a gentle, peaceful path to God-realization while highlighting Guru Nanak's quest for tolerance and compassion. 6 x 9, 192 pp, Quality PB, 978-1-59473-209-6 **$16.99**

Or phone, fax, mail or e-mail to: SKYLIGHT PATHS **Publishing**

Sunset Farm Offices, Route 4 • P.O. Box 237 • Woodstock, Vermont 05091

Tel: (802) 457-4000 • Fax: (802) 457-4004 • www.skylightpaths.com

Credit card orders: (800) 962-4544 (8:30AM–5:30PM ET Monday–Friday)

Generous discounts on quantity orders. SATISFACTION GUARANTEED. Prices subject to change.

Kabbalah from Jewish Lights Publishing

Awakening to Kabbalah: The Guiding Light of Spiritual Fulfillment
by Rav Michael Laitman, PhD 6 x 9, 192 pp, HC, 978-1-58023-264-7 **$21.99**

Cast in God's Image: Discover Your Personality Type Using the Enneagram and Kabbalah
by Rabbi Howard A. Addison 7 x 9, 176 pp, Quality PB, 978-1-58023-124-4 **$16.95**

Ehyeh: A Kabbalah for Tomorrow *by Dr. Arthur Green*
6 x 9, 224 pp, Quality PB, 978-1-58023-213-5 **$16.99**

The Enneagram and Kabbalah, 2nd Edition: Reading Your Soul
by Rabbi Howard A. Addison 6 x 9, 192 pp, Quality PB, 978-1-58023-229-6 **$16.99**

Finding Joy: A Practical Spiritual Guide to Happiness *by Dannel I. Schwartz with Mark Hass*
6 x 9, 192 pp, Quality PB, 978-1-58023-009-4 **$14.95**

The Gift of Kabbalah: Discovering the Secrets of Heaven, Renewing Your Life on Earth
by Tamar Frankiel, PhD 6 x 9, 256 pp, Quality PB, 978-1-58023-141-1 **$16.95**
HC, 978-1-58023-108-4 **$21.95**

Honey from the Rock: An Easy Introduction to Jewish Mysticism
by Lawrence Kushner 6 x 9, 176 pp, Quality PB, 978-1-58023-073-5 **$16.95**

Kabbalah: A Brief Introduction for Christians
by Tamar Frankiel, PhD 5½ x 8½, 176 pp, Quality PB, 978-1-58023-303-3 **$16.99**

Zohar: Annotated & Explained *Translation and Annotation by Dr. Daniel C. Matt*
Foreword by Andrew Harvey 5½ x 8½, 176 pp, Quality PB, 978-1-893361-51-5 **$15.99**

Judaism / Christianity

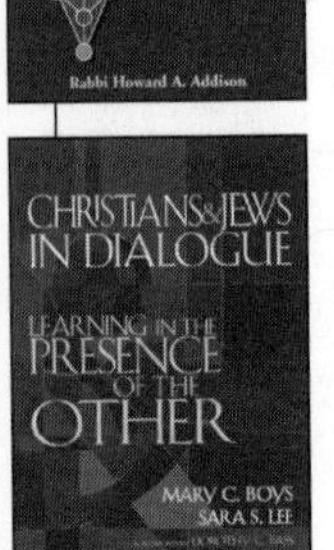

Christians and Jews in Dialogue: Learning in the Presence of the Other
by Mary C. Boys and Sara S. Lee; Foreword by Dorothy C. Bass
Inspires renewed commitment to dialogue between religious traditions and illuminates how it should happen. Explains the transformative work of creating environments for Jews and Christians to study together and enter the dynamism of the other's religious tradition.
6 x 9, 240 pp, HC, 978-1-59473-144-0 **$21.99**

Healing the Jewish-Christian Rift: Growing Beyond Our Wounded History
by Ron Miller and Laura Bernstein; Foreword by Dr. Beatrice Bruteau
6 x 9, 288 pp, Quality PB, 978-1-59473-139-6 **$18.99**

Introducing My Faith and My Community
The Jewish Outreach Institute Guide for the Christian in a Jewish Interfaith Relationship
by Rabbi Kerry M. Olitzky 6 x 9, 176 pp, Quality PB, 978-1-58023-192-3 **$16.99** *(a Jewish Lights book)*

The Jewish Approach to God: A Brief Introduction for Christians
by Rabbi Neil Gillman 5½ x 8½, 192 pp, Quality PB, 978-1-58023-190-9 **$16.95** *(a Jewish Lights book)*

Jewish Holidays: A Brief Introduction for Christians
by Rabbi Kerry M. Olitzky and Rabbi Daniel Judson
5½ x 8½, 176 pp, Quality PB, 978-1-58023-302-6 **$16.99** *(a Jewish Lights book)*

Jewish Ritual: A Brief Introduction for Christians
by Rabbi Kerry M. Olitzky and Rabbi Daniel Judson
5½ x 8½, 144 pp, Quality PB, 978-1-58023-210-4 **$14.99** *(a Jewish Lights book)*

Jewish Spirituality: A Brief Introduction for Christians
by Rabbi Lawrence Kushner
5½ x 8½, 112 pp, Quality PB, 978-1-58023-150-3 **$12.95** *(a Jewish Lights book)*

A Jewish Understanding of the New Testament
by Rabbi Samuel Sandmel; new Preface by Rabbi David Sandmel
5½ x 8½, 368 pp, Quality PB, 978-1-59473-048-1 **$19.99**

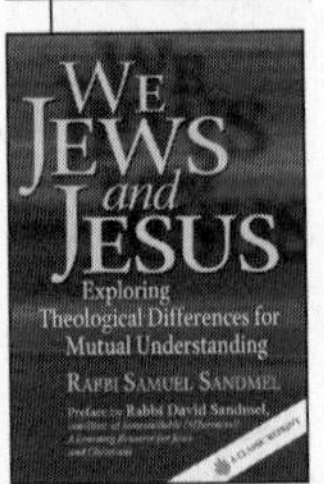

We Jews and Jesus
Exploring Theological Differences for Mutual Understanding
by Rabbi Samuel Sandmel; new Preface by Rabbi David Sandmel A Classic Reprint
Written in a non-technical way for the layperson, this candid and forthright look at the what and why of the Jewish attitude toward Jesus is a clear and forceful exposition that guides both Christians and Jews in relevant discussion.
6 x 9, 192 pp, Quality PB, 978-1-59473-208-9 **$16.99**

Midrash Fiction / Folktales

Abraham's Bind & Other Bible Tales of Trickery, Folly, Mercy and Love *by Michael J. Caduto*
New retellings of episodes in the lives of familiar biblical characters explore relevant life lessons.
6 x 9, 224 pp, HC, 978-1-59473-186-0 **$19.99**

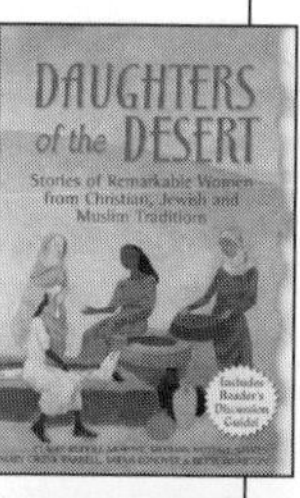

Daughters of the Desert: Stories of Remarkable Women from Christian, Jewish and Muslim Traditions *by Claire Rudolf Murphy, Meghan Nuttall Sayres, Mary Cronk Farrell, Sarah Conover and Betsy Wharton*
Breathes new life into the old tales of our female ancestors in faith. Uses traditional scriptural passages as starting points, then with vivid detail fills in historical context and place. Chapters reveal the voices of Sarah, Hagar, Huldah, Esther, Salome, Mary Magdalene, Lydia, Khadija, Fatima and many more. Historical fiction ideal for readers of all ages. Quality paperback includes reader's discussion guide.
5½ x 8½, 192 pp, Quality PB, 978-1-59473-106-8 **$14.99**
HC, 192 pp, 978-1-893361-72-0 **$19.95**

The Triumph of Eve & Other Subversive Bible Tales
by Matt Biers-Ariel
Many people were taught and remember only a one-dimensional Bible. These engaging retellings are the antidote to this—they're witty, often hilarious, always profound, and invite you to grapple with questions and issues that are often hidden in the original text.
5½ x 8½, 192 pp, Quality PB, 978-1-59473-176-1 **$14.99**
HC, 192 pp, 978-1-59473-040-5 **$19.99**

Also avail.: **The Triumph of Eve Teacher's Guide**
8½ x 11, 44 pp, PB, 978-1-59473-152-5 **$8.99**

Wisdom in the Telling
Finding Inspiration and Grace in Traditional Folktales and Myths Retold
by Lorraine Hartin-Gelardi
6 x 9, 224 pp, HC, 978-1-59473-185-3 **$19.99**

Religious Etiquette / Reference

How to Be a Perfect Stranger, 4th Edition: The Essential Religious Etiquette Handbook *Edited by Stuart M. Matlins and Arthur J. Magida*
The indispensable guidebook to help the well-meaning guest when visiting other people's religious ceremonies. A straightforward guide to the rituals and celebrations of the major religions and denominations in the United States and Canada from the perspective of an interested guest of any other faith, based on information obtained from authorities of each religion. Belongs in every living room, library and office. Covers:
African American Methodist Churches • Assemblies of God • Bahá'í • Baptist • Buddhist • Christian Church (Disciples of Christ) • Christian Science (Church of Christ, Scientist) • Churches of Christ • Episcopalian and Anglican • Hindu • Islam • Jehovah's Witnesses • Jewish • Lutheran • Mennonite/Amish • Methodist • Mormon (Church of Jesus Christ of Latter-day Saints) • Native American/First Nations • Orthodox Churches • Pentecostal Church of God • Presbyterian • Quaker (Religious Society of Friends) • Reformed Church in America/Canada • Roman Catholic • Seventh-day Adventist • Sikh • Unitarian Universalist • United Church of Canada • United Church of Christ
6 x 9, 432 pp, Quality PB, 978-1-59473-140-2 **$19.99**

The Perfect Stranger's Guide to Funerals and Grieving Practices: A Guide to Etiquette in Other People's Religious Ceremonies *Edited by Stuart M. Matlins*
6 x 9, 240 pp, Quality PB, 978-1-893361-20-1 **$16.95**

The Perfect Stranger's Guide to Wedding Ceremonies: A Guide to Etiquette in Other People's Religious Ceremonies *Edited by Stuart M. Matlins*
6 x 9, 208 pp, Quality PB, 978-1-893361-19-5 **$16.95**

Children's Spirituality

ENDORSED BY CATHOLIC, PROTESTANT, JEWISH, AND BUDDHIST RELIGIOUS LEADERS

Adam and Eve's First Sunset: God's New Day
by Sandy Eisenberg Sasso; Full-color illus. by Joani Keller Rothenberg
9 x 12, 32 pp, Full-color illus., HC, 978-1-58023-177-0 **$17.95** *For ages 4 & up (a Jewish Lights book)*

Because Nothing Looks Like God
by Lawrence and Karen Kushner; Full-color illus. by Dawn W. Majewski
Real-life examples of happiness and sadness introduce children to the possibilities of spiritual life. 11 x 8½, 32 pp, HC, Full-color illus., 978-1-58023-092-6 **$16.95** *For ages 4 & up (a Jewish Lights book)*

Also available: **Teacher's Guide,** 8½ x 11, 22 pp, PB, 978-1-58023-140-4 **$6.95** *For ages 5–8*

Becoming Me: A Story of Creation
by Martin Boroson; Full-color illus. by Christopher Gilvan-Cartwright
Told in the personal "voice" of the Creator, a story about creation and relationship that is about each one of us.
8 x 10, 32 pp, Full-color illus., HC, 978-1-893361-11-9 **$16.95** *For ages 4 & up*

But God Remembered: Stories of Women from Creation to the Promised Land *by Sandy Eisenberg Sasso; Full-color illus. by Bethanne Andersen*
A fascinating collection of four different stories of women only briefly mentioned in biblical tradition and religious texts. 9 x 12, 32 pp, HC, Full-color illus., 978-1-879045-43-9 **$16.95**
For ages 8 & up (a Jewish Lights book)

Cain & Abel: Finding the Fruits of Peace
by Sandy Eisenberg Sasso; Full-color illus. by Joani Keller Rothenberg
A sensitive recasting of the ancient tale shows we have the power to deal with anger in positive ways. "Editor's Choice"—American Library Association's *Booklist*
9 x 12, 32 pp, HC, Full-color illus., 978-1-58023-123-7 **$16.95** *For ages 5 & up (a Jewish Lights book)*

Does God Hear My Prayer?
by August Gold; Full-color photos by Diane Hardy Waller
Introduces preschoolers and young readers to prayer and how it helps them express their own emotions. 10 x 8½, 32 pp, Quality PB, Full-color photo illus., 978-1-59473-102-0 **$8.99**

The 11th Commandment: Wisdom from Our Children *by The Children of America*
"If there were an Eleventh Commandment, what would it be?" Children of many religious denominations across America answer this question—in their own drawings and words. "A rare book of spiritual celebration for all people, of all ages, for all time." —*Bookviews*
8 x 10, 48 pp, HC, Full-color illus., 978-1-879045-46-0 **$16.95** *For all ages (a Jewish Lights book)*

For Heaven's Sake *by Sandy Eisenberg Sasso; Full-color illus. by Kathryn Kunz Finney*
Everyone talked about heaven: "Thank heavens." "Heaven forbid." "For heaven's sake, Isaiah." But no one would say what heaven was or how to find it. So Isaiah decides to find out, by seeking answers from many different people.
9 x 12, 32 pp, HC, Full-color illus., 978-1-58023-054-4 **$16.95** *For ages 4 & up (a Jewish Lights book)*

God in Between *by Sandy Eisenberg Sasso; Full-color illus. by Sally Sweetland*
A magical, mythical tale that teaches that God can be found where we are.
9 x 12, 32 pp, HC, Full-color illus., 978-1-879045-86-6 **$16.95** *For ages 4 & up (a Jewish Lights book)*

God's Paintbrush: Special 10th Anniversary Edition
Invites children of all faiths and backgrounds to encounter God through moments in their own lives. 11 x 8½, 32 pp, Full-color illus., HC, 978-1-58023-195-4 **$17.95** *For ages 4 & up*

Also available: **God's Paintbrush Teacher's Guide** 8½ x 11, 32 pp, PB, 978-1-879045-57-6 **$8.95**

God's Paintbrush Celebration Kit
A Spiritual Activity Kit for Teachers and Students of All Faiths, All Backgrounds
Additional activity sheets available:
8-Student Activity Sheet Pack (40 sheets/5 sessions), 978-1-58023-058-2 **$19.95**
Single-Student Activity Sheet Pack (5 sessions), 978-1-58023-059-9 **$3.95**

Children's Spirituality

ENDORSED BY CATHOLIC, PROTESTANT, JEWISH, AND BUDDHIST RELIGIOUS LEADERS

Remembering My Grandparent: A Kid's Own Grief Workbook in the Christian Tradition *by Nechama Liss-Levinson, PhD, and Rev. Molly Phinney Baskette, MDiv*
8 x 10, 48 pp, 2-color text, HC, 978-1-59473-212-6 **$16.99** *For ages 7–13*

Does God Ever Sleep? *by Joan Sauro, CSJ; Full-color photos*
A charming nighttime reminder that God is always present in our lives.
10 x 8½, 32 pp, Quality PB, Full-color photos, 978-1-59473-110-5 **$8.99** *For ages 3–6*

Does God Forgive Me? *by August Gold; Full-color photos by Diane Hardy Waller*
Gently shows how God forgives all that we do if we are truly sorry.
10 x 8½, 32 pp, Quality PB, Full-color photos, 978-1-59473-142-6 **$8.99** *For ages 3–6*

God Said Amen *by Sandy Eisenberg Sasso; Full-color illus. by Avi Katz*
A warm and inspiring tale of two kingdoms that shows us that we need only reach out to each other to find the answers to our prayers.
9 x 12, 32 pp, HC, Full-color illus., 978-1-58023-080-3 **$16.95**
For ages 4 & up (a Jewish Lights book)

How Does God Listen? *by Kay Lindahl; Full-color photos by Cynthia Maloney*
How do we know when God is listening to us? Children will find the answers to these questions as they engage their senses while the story unfolds, learning how God listens in the wind, waves, clouds, hot chocolate, perfume, our tears and our laughter.
10 x 8½, 32 pp, Quality PB, Full-color photos, 978-1-59473-084-9 **$8.99** *For ages 3–6*

In God's Hands *by Lawrence Kushner and Gary Schmidt; Full-color illus. by Matthew J. Baeck*
9 x 12, 32 pp, Full-color illus., HC, 978-1-58023-224-1 **$16.99** *For ages 5 & up (a Jewish Lights book)*

In God's Name *by Sandy Eisenberg Sasso; Full-color illus. by Phoebe Stone*
Like an ancient myth in its poetic text and vibrant illustrations, this award-winning modern fable about the search for God's name celebrates the diversity and, at the same time, the unity of all the people of the world.
9 x 12, 32 pp, HC, Full-color illus., 978-1-879045-26-2 **$16.99**
For ages 4 & up (a Jewish Lights book)

Also available in Spanish: **El nombre de Dios**
9 x 12, 32 pp, HC, Full-color illus., 978-1-893361-63-8 **$16.95**

In Our Image: God's First Creatures
by Nancy Sohn Swartz; Full-color illus. by Melanie Hall
A playful new twist on the Genesis story—from the perspective of the animals. Celebrates the interconnectedness of nature and the harmony of all living things. 9 x 12, 32 pp, HC, Full-color illus., 978-1-879045-99-6 **$16.95**
For ages 4 & up (a Jewish Lights book)

Noah's Wife: The Story of Naamah
by Sandy Eisenberg Sasso; Full-color illus. by Bethanne Andersen
This new story, based on an ancient text, opens readers' religious imaginations to new ideas about the well-known story of the Flood. When God tells Noah to bring the animals of the world onto the ark, God also calls on Naamah, Noah's wife, to save each plant on Earth.
9 x 12, 32 pp, HC, Full-color illus., 978-1-58023-134-3 **$16.95**
For ages 4 & up (a Jewish Lights book)

Also available: **Naamah:** Noah's Wife (A Board Book)
by Sandy Eisenberg Sasso; Full-color illus. by Bethanne Andersen
5 x 5, 24 pp, Board Book, Full-color illus., 978-1-893361-56-0 **$7.99** *For ages 0–4*

Where Does God Live? *by August Gold and Matthew J. Perlman*
Using simple, everyday examples that children can relate to, this colorful book helps young readers develop a personal understanding of God.
10 x 8½, 32 pp, Quality PB, Full-color photo illus., 978-1-893361-39-3 **$8.99** *For ages 3–6*

Children's Spirituality—Board Books

Adam and Eve's New Day (A Board Book)
by Sandy Eisenberg Sasso; Full-color illus. by Joani Keller Rothenberg
A lesson in hope for every child who has worried about what comes next. Abridged from *Adam and Eve's First Sunset.*
5 x 5, 24 pp, Full-color illus., Board Book, 978-1-59473-205-8 **$7.99** *For ages 0–4*

How Did the Animals Help God? (A Board Book)
by Nancy Sohn Swartz; Full-color illus. by Melanie Hall
Abridged from *In Our Image,* God asks all of nature to offer gifts to humankind—with a promise that they will care for creation in return.
5 x 5, 24 pp, Board Book, Full-color illus., 978-1-59473-044-3 **$7.99** *For ages 0–4*

Where Is God? (A Board Book) *by Lawrence and Karen Kushner; Full-color illus. by Dawn W. Majewski* A gentle way for young children to explore how God is with us every day, in every way. Abridged from *Because Nothing Looks Like God.*
5 x 5, 24 pp, Board Book, Full-color illus., 978-1-893361-17-1 **$7.99** *For ages 0–4*

What Does God Look Like? (A Board Book)
by Lawrence and Karen Kushner; Full-color illus. by Dawn W. Majewski
A simple way for young children to explore the ways that we "see" God. Abridged from *Because Nothing Looks Like God.*
5 x 5, 24 pp, Board Book, Full-color illus., 978-1-893361-23-2 **$7.95** *For ages 0–4*

How Does God Make Things Happen? (A Board Book)
by Lawrence and Karen Kushner; Full-color illus. by Dawn W. Majewski
A charming invitation for young children to explore how God makes things happen in our world. Abridged from *Because Nothing Looks Like God.*
5 x 5, 24 pp, Board Book, Full-color illus., 978-1-893361-24-9 **$7.95** *For ages 0–4*

What Is God's Name? (A Board Book)
by Sandy Eisenberg Sasso; Full-color illus. by Phoebe Stone
Everyone and everything in the world has a name. What is God's name? Abridged from the award-winning *In God's Name.*
5 x 5, 24 pp, Board Book, Full-color illus., 978-1-893361-10-2 **$7.99** *For ages 0–4*

What You Will See Inside …

This important new series of books, each with many full-color photos, is designed to show children ages 6 and up the Who, What, When, Where, Why and How of traditional houses of worship, liturgical celebrations, and rituals of different world faiths, empowering them to respect and understand their own religious traditions—and those of their friends and neighbors.

What You Will See Inside a Catholic Church
by Reverend Michael Keane; Foreword by Robert J. Keeley, EdD
Full-color photos by Aaron Pepis
8½ x 10½, 32 pp, Full-color photos, HC, 978-1-893361-54-6 **$17.95**
Also available in Spanish: **Lo que se puede ver dentro de una iglesia católica**
8½ x 10½, 32 pp, Full-color photos, HC, 978-1-893361-66-9 **$16.95**

What You Will See Inside a Hindu Temple
by Dr. Mahendra Jani and Dr. Vandana Jani; Full-color photos by Neirah Bhargava and Vijay Dave
8½ x 10½, 32 pp, Full-color photos, HC, 978-1-59473-116-7 **$17.99**

What You Will See Inside a Mosque
by Aisha Karen Khan; Full-color photos by Aaron Pepis
8½ x 10½, 32 pp, Full-color photos, HC, 978-1-893361-60-7 **$16.95**

What You Will See Inside a Synagogue
by Rabbi Lawrence A. Hoffman and Dr. Ron Wolfson; Full-color photos by Bill Aron
8½ x 10½, 32 pp, Full-color photos, HC, 978-1-59473-012-2 **$17.99**

Children's Spiritual Biography

MULTICULTURAL, NONDENOMINATIONAL, NONSECTARIAN

Ten Amazing People

And How They Changed the World

by Maura D. Shaw; Foreword by Dr. Robert Coles

Full-color illus. by Stephen Marchesi

For ages 7 & up

Black Elk • Dorothy Day • Malcolm X • Mahatma Gandhi • Martin Luther King, Jr. • Mother Teresa • Janusz Korczak • Desmond Tutu • Thich Nhat Hanh • Albert Schweitzer

This vivid, inspirational and authoritative book will open new possibilities for children by telling the stories of how ten of the past century's greatest leaders changed the world in important ways.

8½ x 11, 48 pp, HC, Full-color illus., 978-1-893361-47-8 **$17.95**

For ages 7 & up

Spiritual Biographies for Young People—For ages 7 and up

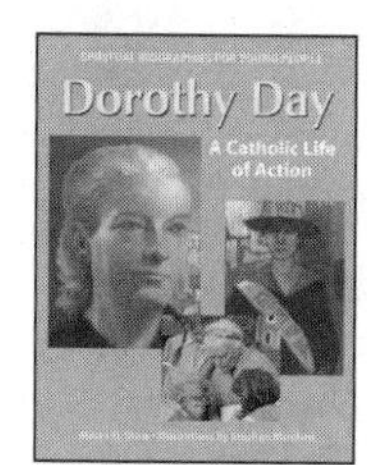

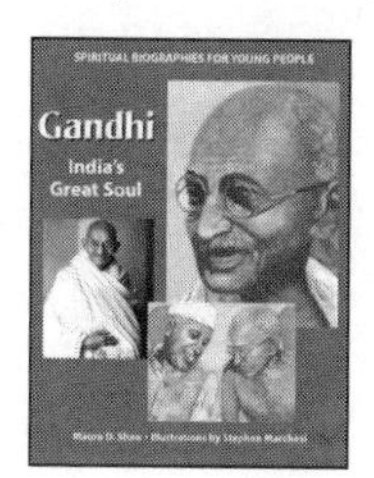

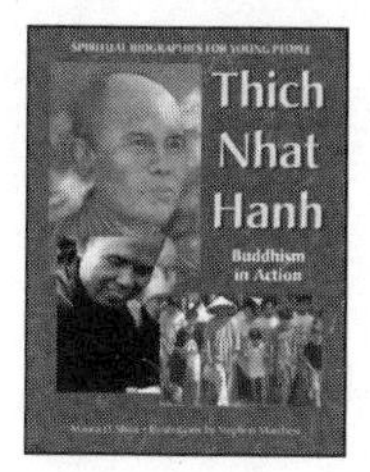

Black Elk: Native American Man of Spirit

by Maura D. Shaw; Full-color illus. by Stephen Marchesi

Through historically accurate illustrations and photos, inspiring age-appropriate activities and Black Elk's own words, this colorful biography introduces children to a remarkable person who ensured that the traditions and beliefs of his people would not be forgotten.

6¾ x 8¾, 32 pp, HC, Full-color and b/w illus., 978-1-59473-043-6 **$12.99**

Dorothy Day: A Catholic Life of Action

by Maura D. Shaw; Full-color illus. by Stephen Marchesi

Introduces children to one of the most inspiring women of the twentieth century, a down-to-earth spiritual leader who saw the presence of God in every person she met. Includes practical activities, a timeline and a list of important words to know.

6¾ x 8¾, 32 pp, HC, Full-color illus., 978-1-59473-011-5 **$12.99**

Gandhi: India's Great Soul

by Maura D. Shaw; Full-color illus. by Stephen Marchesi

There are a number of biographies of Gandhi written for young readers, but this is the only one that balances a simple text with illustrations, photographs, and activities that encourage children and adults to talk about how to make changes happen without violence. Introduces children to important concepts of freedom, equality and justice among people of all backgrounds and religions.

6¾ x 8¾, 32 pp, HC, Full-color illus., 978-1-893361-91-1 **$12.95**

Thich Nhat Hanh: Buddhism in Action

by Maura D. Shaw; Full-color illus. by Stephen Marchesi

Warm illustrations, photos, age-appropriate activities and Thich Nhat Hanh's own poems introduce a great man to children in a way they can understand and enjoy. Includes a list of important Buddhist words to know.

6¾ x 8¾, 32 pp, HC, Full-color illus., 978-1-893361-87-4 **$12.95**

Sacred Texts—SkyLight Illuminations Series

Offers today's spiritual seeker an accessible entry into the great classic texts of the world's spiritual traditions. Each classic is presented in an accessible translation, with facing pages of guided commentary from experts, giving you the keys you need to understand the history, context and meaning of the text. This series enables you, whatever your background, to experience and understand classic spiritual texts directly, and to make them a part of your life.

CHRISTIANITY

The End of Days: Essential Selections from Apocalyptic Texts—Annotated & Explained *Annotation by Robert G. Clouse*
Helps you understand the complex Christian visions of the end of the world.
5½ x 8½, 224 pp, Quality PB, 978-1-59473-170-9 **$16.99**

The Hidden Gospel of Matthew: Annotated & Explained
Translation & Annotation by Ron Miller
Takes you deep into the text cherished around the world to discover the words and events that have the strongest connection to the historical Jesus.
5½ x 8½, 272 pp, Quality PB, 978-1-59473-038-2 **$16.99**

The Lost Sayings of Jesus: Teachings from Ancient Christian, Jewish, Gnostic and Islamic Sources—Annotated & Explained
Translation & Annotation by Andrew Phillip Smith; Foreword by Stephan A. Hoeller
This collection of more than three hundred sayings depicts Jesus as a Wisdom teacher who speaks to people of all faiths as a mystic and spiritual master.
5½ x 8½, 240 pp, Quality PB, 978-1-59473-172-3 **$16.99**

Philokalia: The Eastern Christian Spiritual Texts—Selections Annotated & Explained *Annotation by Allyne Smith; Translation by G. E. H. Palmer, Phillip Sherrard and Bishop Kallistos Ware*
The first approachable introduction to the wisdom of the Philokalia, which is the classic text of Eastern Christian spirituality.
5½ x 8½, 240 pp, Quality PB, 978-1-59473-103-7 **$16.99**

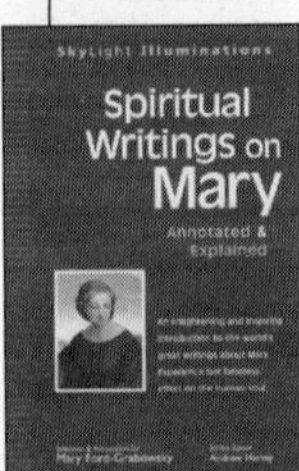

Spiritual Writings on Mary: Annotated & Explained
Annotation by Mary Ford-Grabowsky; Foreword by Andrew Harvey
Examines the role of Mary, the mother of Jesus, as a source of inspiration in history and in life today. 5½ x 8½, 288 pp, Quality PB, 978-1-59473-001-6 **$16.99**

The Way of a Pilgrim: The Jesus Prayer Journey—Annotated & Explained
Translation & Annotation by Gleb Pokrovsky; Foreword by Andrew Harvey
This classic of Russian spirituality is the delightful account of one man who sets out to learn the prayer of the heart, also known as the "Jesus prayer."
5½ x 8½, 160 pp, Illus., Quality PB, 978-1-893361-31-7 **$14.95**

MORMONISM

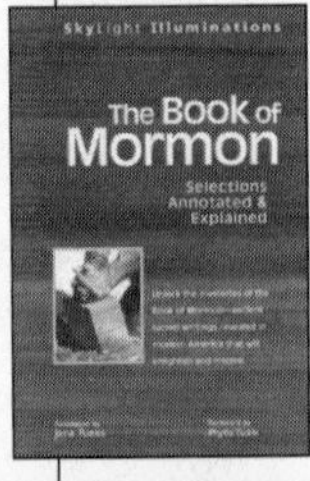

The Book of Mormon: Selections Annotated & Explained
Annotation by Jana Riess; Foreword by Phyllis Tickle
Explores the sacred epic that is cherished by more than twelve million members of the LDS church as the keystone of their faith.
5½ x 8½ , 272 pp, Quality PB, 978-1-59473-076-4 **$16.99**

NATIVE AMERICAN

Native American Stories of the Sacred: Annotated & Explained
Retold & Annotated by Evan T. Pritchard
Intended for more than entertainment, these teaching tales contain elegantly simple illustrations of time-honored truths.
5½ x 8½, 272 pp, Quality PB, 978-1-59473-112-9 **$16.99**

Sacred Texts—cont.

GNOSTICISM

The Gospel of Philip: Annotated & Explained
Translation & Annotation by Andrew Phillip Smith; Foreword by Stevan Davies
Reveals otherwise unrecorded sayings of Jesus and fragments of Gnostic mythology.
5½ x 8½, 160 pp, Quality PB, 978-1-59473-111-2 **$16.99**

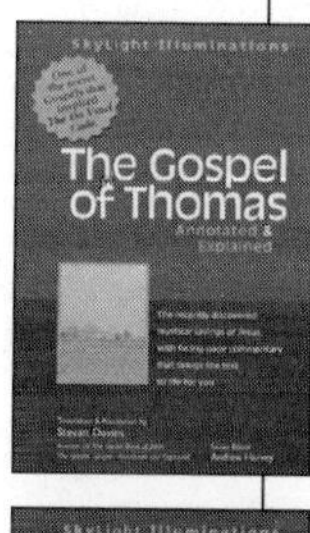

The Gospel of Thomas: Annotated & Explained
Translation & Annotation by Stevan Davies Sheds new light on the origins of Christianity and portrays Jesus as a wisdom-loving sage. 5½ x 8½, 192 pp, Quality PB, 978-1-893361-45-4 **$16.99**

The Secret Book of John: The Gnostic Gospel—Annotated & Explained
Translation & Annotation by Stevan Davies The most significant and influential text of the ancient Gnostic religion. 5½ x 8½, 208 pp, Quality PB, 978-1-59473-082-5 **$16.99**

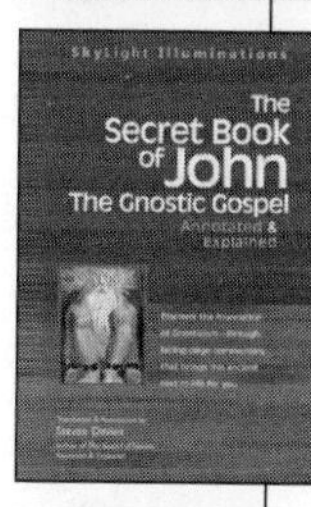

JUDAISM

The Divine Feminine in Biblical Wisdom Literature
Selections Annotated & Explained
Translation & Annotation by Rabbi Rami Shapiro; Foreword by Rev. Cynthia Bourgeault, PhD
Uses the Hebrew books of Psalms, Proverbs, Song of Songs, Ecclesiastes and Job, Wisdom literature and the Wisdom of Solomon to clarify who Wisdom is.
5½ x 8½, 240 pp, Quality PB, 978-1-59473-109-9 **$16.99**

Ethics of the Sages: *Pirke Avot*—Annotated & Explained
Translation & Annotation by Rabbi Rami Shapiro Clarifies the ethical teachings of the early Rabbis. 5½ x 8½, 192 pp, Quality PB, 978-1-59473-207-2 **$16.99**

Hasidic Tales: Annotated & Explained
Translation & Annotation by Rabbi Rami Shapiro
Introduces the legendary tales of the impassioned Hasidic rabbis, presenting them as stories rather than as parables. 5½ x 8½, 240 pp, Quality PB, 978-1-893361-86-7 **$16.95**

The Hebrew Prophets: Selections Annotated & Explained
Translation & Annotation by Rabbi Rami Shapiro; Foreword by Zalman M. Schachter-Shalomi
Focuses on the central themes covered by all the Hebrew prophets.
5½ x 8½, 224 pp, Quality PB, 978-1-59473-037-5 **$16.99**

Zohar: Annotated & Explained *Translation & Annotation by Daniel C. Matt*
The best-selling author of *The Essential Kabbalah* brings together in one place the most important teachings of the Zohar, the canonical text of Jewish mystical tradition.
5½ x 8½, 176 pp, Quality PB, 978-1-893361-51-5 **$15.99**

EASTERN RELIGIONS

Bhagavad Gita: Annotated & Explained *Translation by Shri Purohit Swami*
Annotation by Kendra Crossen Burroughs Explains references and philosophical terms, shares the interpretations of famous spiritual leaders and scholars, and more.
5½ x 8½, 192 pp, Quality PB, 978-1-893361-28-7 **$16.95**

Dhammapada: Annotated & Explained *Translation by Max Müller and revised by Jack Maguire; Annotation by Jack Maguire* Contains all of Buddhism's key teachings.
5½ x 8½, 160 pp, b/w photos, Quality PB, 978-1-893361-42-3 **$14.95**

Rumi and Islam: Selections from His Stories, Poems, and Discourses—Annotated & Explained *Translation & Annotation by Ibrahim Gamard*
Focuses on Rumi's place within the Sufi tradition of Islam, providing insight into the mystical side of the religion. 5½ x 8½, 240 pp, Quality PB, 978-1-59473-002-3 **$15.99**

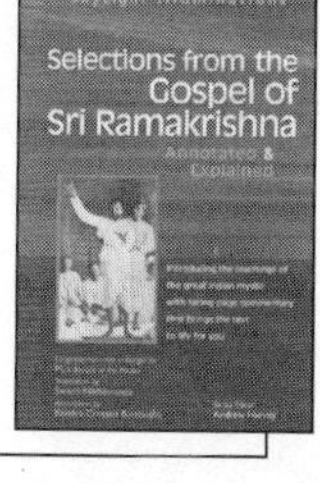

Selections from the Gospel of Sri Ramakrishna: Annotated & Explained
Translation by Swami Nikhilananda; Annotation by Kendra Crossen Burroughs
Introduces the fascinating world of the Indian mystic and the universal appeal of his message. 5½ x 8½, 240 pp, b/w photos, Quality PB, 978-1-893361-46-1 **$16.95**

Tao Te Ching: Annotated & Explained *Translation & Annotation by Derek Lin*
Foreword by Lama Surya Das Introduces an Eastern classic in an accessible, poetic and completely original way. 5½ x 8½, 192 pp, Quality PB, 978-1-59473-204-1 **$16.99**

Spiritual Biography—SkyLight Lives

SkyLight Lives reintroduces the lives and works of key spiritual figures of our time—people who by their teaching or example have challenged our assumptions about spirituality and have caused us to look at it in new ways.

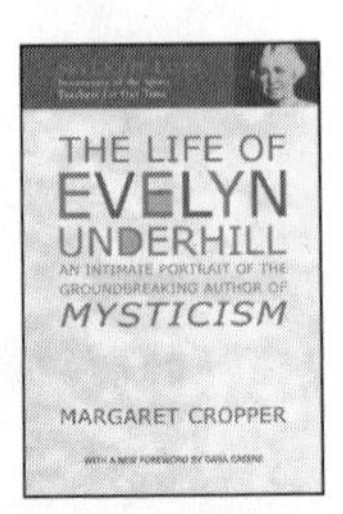

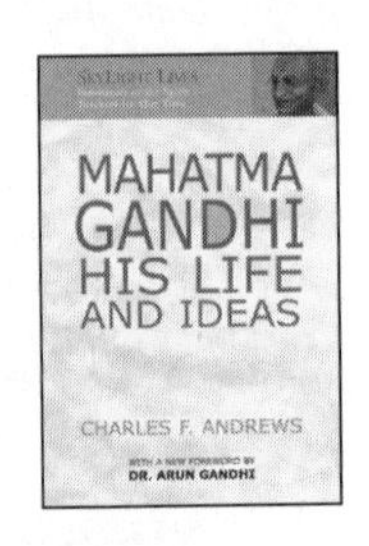

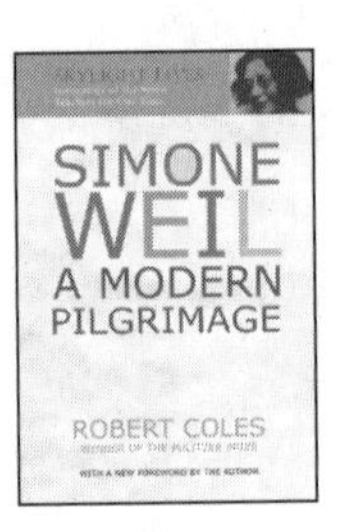

The Life of Evelyn Underhill
An Intimate Portrait of the Groundbreaking Author of *Mysticism*
by Margaret Cropper; Foreword by Dana Greene
Evelyn Underhill was a passionate writer and teacher who wrote elegantly on mysticism, worship, and devotional life.
6 x 9, 288 pp, 5 b/w photos, Quality PB, 978-1-893361-70-6 **$18.95**

Mahatma Gandhi: His Life and Ideas
by Charles F. Andrews; Foreword by Dr. Arun Gandhi
Examines from a contemporary Christian activist's point of view the religious ideas and political dynamics that influenced the birth of the peaceful resistance movement.
6 x 9, 336 pp, 5 b/w photos, Quality PB, 978-1-893361-89-8 **$18.95**

Simone Weil: A Modern Pilgrimage
by Robert Coles
The extraordinary life of the spiritual philosopher who's been called both saint and madwoman.
6 x 9, 208 pp, Quality PB, 978-1-893361-34-8 **$16.95**

Zen Effects: The Life of Alan Watts
by Monica Furlong
Through his widely popular books and lectures, Alan Watts (1915–1973) did more to introduce Eastern philosophy and religion to Western minds than any figure before or since.
6 x 9, 264 pp, Quality PB, 978-1-893361-32-4 **$16.95**

More Spiritual Biography

Bede Griffiths: An Introduction to His Interspiritual Thought
by Wayne Teasdale
The first study of his contemplative experience and thought, exploring the intersection of Hinduism and Christianity.
6 x 9, 288 pp, Quality PB, 978-1-893361-77-5 **$18.95**

The Soul of the Story: Meetings with Remarkable People
by Rabbi David Zeller
Inspiring and entertaining, this compelling collection of spiritual adventures assures us that no spiritual lesson truly learned is ever lost.
6 x 9, 288 pp, HC, 978-1-58023-272-2 **$21.99** *(a Jewish Lights book)*

Spiritual Poetry—The Mystic Poets

Experience these mystic poets as you never have before. Each beautiful, compact book includes: a brief introduction to the poet's time and place; a summary of the major themes of the poet's mysticism and religious tradition; essential selections from the poet's most important works; and an appreciative preface by a contemporary spiritual writer.

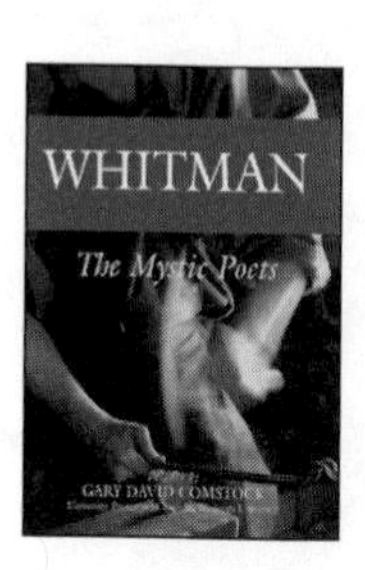

Hafiz: The Mystic Poets
Preface by Ibrahim Gamard
Hafiz is known throughout the world as Persia's greatest poet, with sales of his poems in Iran today only surpassed by those of the Qur'an itself. His probing and joyful verse speaks to people from all backgrounds who long to taste and feel divine love and experience harmony with all living things.
5 x 7¼, 144 pp, HC, 978-1-59473-009-2 **$16.99**

Hopkins: The Mystic Poets
Preface by Rev. Thomas Ryan, CSP
Gerard Manley Hopkins, Christian mystical poet, is beloved for his use of fresh language and startling metaphors to describe the world around him. Although his verse is lovely, beneath the surface lies a searching soul, wrestling with and yearning for God.
5 x 7¼, 112 pp, HC, 978-1-59473-010-8 **$16.99**

Tagore: The Mystic Poets
Preface by Swami Adiswarananda
Rabindranath Tagore is often considered the "Shakespeare" of modern India. A great mystic, Tagore was the teacher of W. B. Yeats and Robert Frost, the close friend of Albert Einstein and Mahatma Gandhi, and the winner of the Nobel Prize for Literature. This beautiful sampling of Tagore's two most important works, *The Gardener* and *Gitanjali,* offers a glimpse into his spiritual vision that has inspired people around the world.
5 x 7¼, 144 pp, HC, 978-1-59473-008-5 **$16.99**

Whitman: The Mystic Poets
Preface by Gary David Comstock
Walt Whitman was the most innovative and influential poet of the nineteenth century. This beautiful sampling of Whitman's most important poetry from *Leaves of Grass,* and selections from his prose writings, offers a glimpse into the spiritual side of his most radical themes—love for country, love for others, and love of Self.
5 x 7¼, 192 pp, HC, 978-1-59473-041-2 **$16.99**

Spirituality of the Seasons

Autumn: A Spiritual Biography of the Season
Edited by Gary Schmidt and Susan M. Felch; Illustrations by Mary Azarian
Rejoice in autumn as a time of preparation and reflection. Includes Wendell Berry, David James Duncan, Robert Frost, A. Bartlett Giamatti, E. B. White, P. D. James, Julian of Norwich, Garret Keizer, Tracy Kidder, Anne Lamott, May Sarton.
6 x 9, 320 pp, 5 b/w illus., Quality PB, 978-1-59473-118-1 **$18.99**
HC, 978-1-59473-005-4 **$22.99**

Spring: A Spiritual Biography of the Season
Edited by Gary Schmidt and Susan M. Felch; Illustrations by Mary Azarian
Explore the gentle unfurling of spring and reflect on how nature celebrates rebirth and renewal. Includes Jane Kenyon, Lucy Larcom, Harry Thurston, Nathaniel Hawthorne, Noel Perrin, Annie Dillard, Martha Ballard, Barbara Kingsolver, Dorothy Wordsworth, Donald Hall, David Brill, Lionel Basney, Isak Dinesen, Paul Laurence Dunbar. 6 x 9, 352 pp, 6 b/w illus., HC, 978-1-59473-114-3 **$21.99**

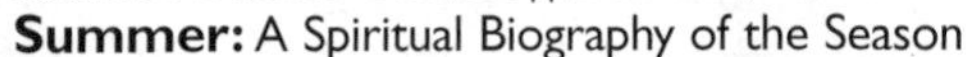

Summer: A Spiritual Biography of the Season
Edited by Gary Schmidt and Susan M. Felch; Illustrations by Barry Moser
"A sumptuous banquet.... These selections lift up an exquisite wholeness found within an everyday sophistication."— ★ *Publishers Weekly* starred review
Includes Anne Lamott, Luci Shaw, Ray Bradbury, Richard Selzer, Thomas Lynch, Walt Whitman, Carl Sandburg, Sherman Alexie, Madeleine L'Engle, Jamaica Kincaid.
6 x 9, 304 pp, 5 b/w illus., Quality PB, 978-1-59473-183-9 **$18.99**
HC, 978-1-59473-083-2 **$21.99**

Winter: A Spiritual Biography of the Season
Edited by Gary Schmidt and Susan M. Felch; Illustrations by Barry Moser
"This outstanding anthology features top-flight nature and spirituality writers on the fierce, inexorable season of winter.... Remarkably lively and warm, despite the icy subject." — ★ *Publishers Weekly* starred review.
Includes Will Campbell, Rachel Carson, Annie Dillard, Donald Hall, Ron Hansen, Jane Kenyon, Jamaica Kincaid, Barry Lopez, Kathleen Norris, John Updike, E. B. White.
6 x 9, 288 pp, 6 b/w illus., Deluxe PB w/flaps, 978-1-893361-92-8 **$18.95**
HC, 978-1-893361-53-9 **$21.95**

Spirituality / Animal Companions

Blessing the Animals: Prayers and Ceremonies to Celebrate God's Creatures, Wild and Tame *Edited by Lynn L. Caruso* 5 x 7¼, 256 pp, HC, 978-1-59473-145-7 **$19.99**

What Animals Can Teach Us about Spirituality: Inspiring Lessons from Wild and Tame Creatures *by Diana L. Guerrero* 6 x 9, 176 pp, Quality PB, 978-1-893361-84-3 **$16.95**

Spirituality

Awakening the Spirit, Inspiring the Soul
30 Stories of Interspiritual Discovery in the Community of Faiths
Edited by Brother Wayne Teasdale and Martha Howard, MD; Foreword by Joan Borysenko, PhD
Thirty original spiritual mini-autobiographies showcase the varied ways that people come to faith—and what that means—in today's multi-religious world.
6 x 9, 224 pp, HC, 978-1-59473-039-9 **$21.99**

The Alphabet of Paradise: An A–Z of Spirituality for Everyday Life *by Howard Cooper* 5 x 7¾, 224 pp, Quality PB, 978-1-893361-80-5 **$16.95**

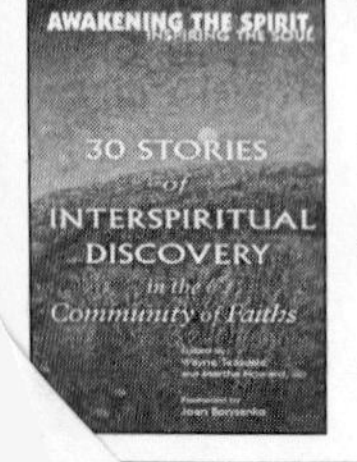

Creating a Spiritual Retirement: A Guide to the Unseen Possibilities in Our Lives *by Molly Srode* 6 x 9, 208 pp, b/w photos, Quality PB, 978-1-59473-050-4 **$14.99**
HC, 978-1-893361-75-1 **$19.95**

Finding Hope: Cultivating God's Gift of a Hopeful Spirit *by Marcia Ford* 8 x 8, 200 pp, Quality PB, 978-1-59473-211-9 **$16.99**

The Geography of Faith: Underground Conversations on Religious, Political and Social Change *by Daniel Berrigan and Robert Coles* 6 x 9, 224 pp, Quality PB, 978-1-893361-40-9 **$16.95**

God Within: Our Spiritual Future—As Told by Today's New Adults *Edited by Jon M. Sweeney and the Editors at SkyLight Paths* 6 x 9, 176 pp, Quality PB, 978-1-893361-15-7 **$14.95**

Spirituality

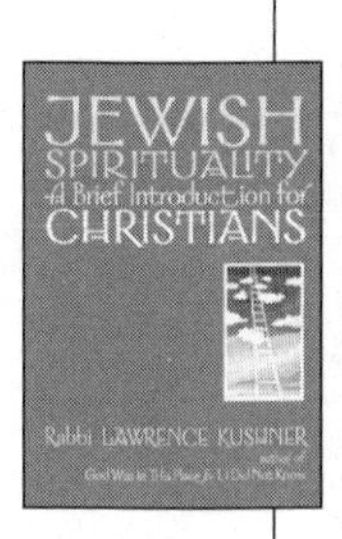

Jewish Spirituality: A Brief Introduction for Christians *by Lawrence Kushner*
5½ x 8½, 112 pp, Quality PB, 978-1-58023-150-3 **$12.95** *(a Jewish Lights book)*

Journeys of Simplicity: Traveling Light with Thomas Merton, Bashō, Edward Abbey, Annie Dillard & Others *by Philip Harnden* 5 x 7¼, 144 pp, Quality PB, 978-1-59473-181-5 **$12.99**
128 pp, HC, 978-1-893361-76-8 **$16.95**

Keeping Spiritual Balance As We Grow Older: More than 65 Creative Ways to Use Purpose, Prayer, and the Power of Spirit to Build a Meaningful Retirement
by Molly and Bernie Srode 8 x 8, 224 pp, Quality PB, 978-1-59473-042-9 **$16.99**

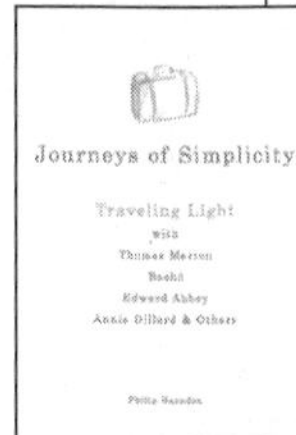

The Monks of Mount Athos: A Western Monk's Extraordinary Spiritual Journey on Eastern Holy Ground *by M. Basil Pennington, ocso; Foreword by Archimandrite Dionysios*
6 x 9, 256 pp, 10+ b/w line drawings, Quality PB, 978-1-893361-78-2 **$18.95**

One God Clapping: The Spiritual Path of a Zen Rabbi *by Alan Lew with Sherrill Jaffe*
5½ x 8½, 336 pp, Quality PB, 978-1-58023-115-2 **$16.95** *(a Jewish Lights book)*

Prayer for People Who Think Too Much: A Guide to Everyday, Anywhere Prayer from the World's Faith Traditions *by Mitch Finley*
5½ x 8½, 224 pp, Quality PB, 978-1-893361-21-8 **$16.99**; HC, 978-1-893361-00-3 **$21.95**

Show Me Your Way: The Complete Guide to Exploring Interfaith Spiritual Direction
by Howard A. Addison 5½ x 8½, 240 pp, Quality PB, 978-1-893361-41-6 **$16.95**

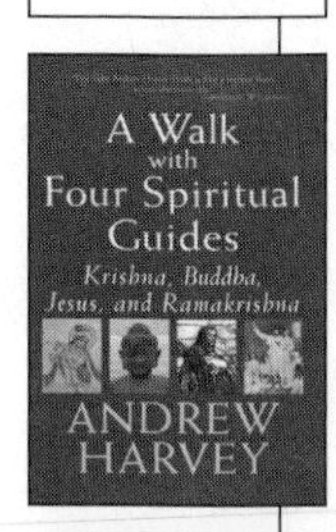

Spirituality 101: The Indispensable Guide to Keeping—or Finding—Your Spiritual Life on Campus *by Harriet L. Schwartz, with contributions from college students at nearly thirty campuses across the United States* 6 x 9, 272 pp, Quality PB, 978-1-59473-000-9 **$16.99**

Spiritually Incorrect: Finding God in All the *Wrong* Places *by Dan Wakefield; Illus. by Marian DelVecchio* 5½ x 8½, 192 pp, b/w illus., Quality PB, 978-1-59473-137-2 **$15.99**

Spiritual Manifestos: Visions for Renewed Religious Life in America from Young Spiritual Leaders of Many Faiths *Edited by Niles Elliot Goldstein; Preface by Martin E. Marty*
6 x 9, 256 pp, HC, 978-1-893361-09-6 **$21.95**

A Walk with Four Spiritual Guides: Krishna, Buddha, Jesus, and Ramakrishna
by Andrew Harvey 5½ x 8½, 192 pp, 10 b/w photos & illus., Quality PB, 978-1-59473-138-9 **$15.99**

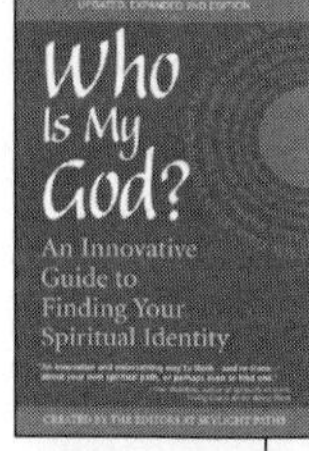

What Matters: Spiritual Nourishment for Head and Heart
by Frederick Franck 5 x 7¼, 128 pp, 50+ b/w illus., HC, 978-1-59473-013-9 **$16.99**

Who Is My God?, 2nd Edition: An Innovative Guide to Finding Your Spiritual Identity
Created by the Editors at SkyLight Paths 6 x 9, 160 pp, Quality PB, 978-1-59473-014-6 **$15.99**

Spirituality—A Week Inside

Come and Sit: A Week Inside Meditation Centers
by Marcia Z. Nelson; Foreword by Wayne Teasdale
The insider's guide to meditation in a variety of different spiritual traditions—Buddhist, Hindu, Christian, Jewish, and Sufi traditions.
6 x 9, 224 pp, b/w photos, Quality PB, 978-1-893361-35-5 **$16.95**

Lighting the Lamp of Wisdom: A Week Inside a Yoga Ashram
by John Ittner; Foreword by Dr. David Frawley
This insider's guide to Hindu spiritual life takes you into a typical week of retreat inside a yoga ashram to demystify the experience and show you what to expect.
6 x 9, 192 pp, 10+ b/w photos, Quality PB, 978-1-893361-52-2 **$15.95**

Making a Heart for God: A Week Inside a Catholic Monastery
by Dianne Aprile; Foreword by Brother Patrick Hart, ocso
Takes you to the Abbey of Gethsemani—the Trappist monastery in Kentucky that was home to author Thomas Merton—to explore the details.
6 x 9, 224 pp, b/w photos, Quality PB, 978-1-893361-49-2 **$16.95**

Waking Up: A Week Inside a Zen Monastery
by Jack Maguire; Foreword by John Daido Loori, Roshi
An essential guide to what it's like to spend a week inside a Zen Buddhist monastery.
6 x 9, 224 pp, b/w photos, Quality PB, 978-1-893361-55-3 **$16.95**
HC, 978-1-893361-13-3 **$21.95**

Spirituality & Crafts

The Knitting Way: A Guide to Spiritual Self-Discovery
by Linda Skolnik and Janice MacDaniels
7 x 9, 240 pp, Quality PB, b/w photographs, 978-1-59473-079-5 **$16.99**

The Quilting Path: A Guide to Spiritual Discovery through Fabric, Thread and Kabbalah
by Louise Silk
7 x 9, 192 pp, Quality PB, b/w photographs and illustrations, 978-1-59473-206-5 **$16.99**

The Scrapbooking Journey: A Hands-On Guide to Spiritual Discovery
by Cory Richardson-Lauve; Foreword by Stacy Julian
7 x 9, 176 pp, Quality PB, 8-page full-color insert, plus b/w photographs
978-1-59473-216-4 **$18.99**

Spiritual Practice

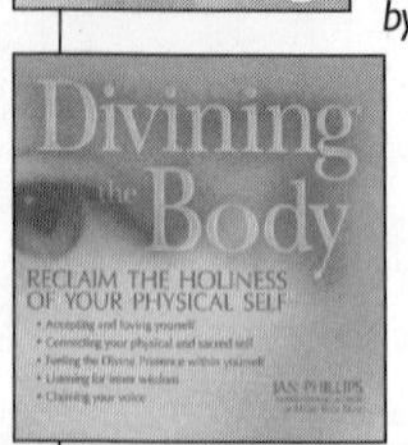

Divining the Body: Reclaim the Holiness of Your Physical Self
by Jan Phillips
A practical and inspiring guidebook for connecting the body and soul in spiritual practice. Leads you into a milieu of reverence, mystery and delight, helping you discover your body as a pathway to the Divine.
8 x 8, 256 pp, Quality PB, 978-1-59473-080-1 **$16.99**

Finding Time for the Timeless: Spirituality in the Workweek
by John McQuiston II
Simple, refreshing stories that provide you with examples of how you can refocus and enrich your daily life using prayer or meditation, ritual and other forms of spiritual practice. 5½ x 6¾, 208 pp, HC, 978-1-59473-035-1 **$17.99**

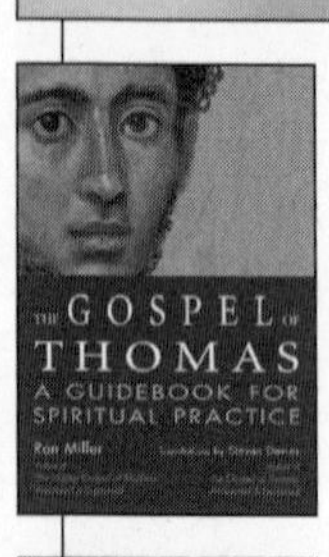

The Gospel of Thomas: A Guidebook for Spiritual Practice
by Ron Miller; Translations by Stevan Davies
An innovative guide to bring a new spiritual classic into daily life.
6 x 9, 160 pp, Quality PB, 978-1-59473-047-4 **$14.99**

Earth, Water, Fire, and Air: Essential Ways of Connecting to Spirit
by Cait Johnson 6 x 9, 224 pp, HC, 978-1-893361-65-2 **$19.95**

Labyrinths from the Outside In: Walking to Spiritual Insight—A Beginner's Guide
by Donna Schaper and Carole Ann Camp
6 x 9, 208 pp, b/w illus. and photos, Quality PB, 978-1-893361-18-8 **$16.95**

Practicing the Sacred Art of Listening: A Guide to Enrich Your Relationships and Kindle Your Spiritual Life—The Listening Center Workshop
by Kay Lindahl 8 x 8, 176 pp, Quality PB, 978-1-893361-85-0 **$16.95**

Releasing the Creative Spirit: Unleash the Creativity in Your Life
by Dan Wakefield 7 x 10, 256 pp, Quality PB, 978-1-893361-36-2 **$16.95**

The Sacred Art of Bowing: Preparing to Practice
by Andi Young 5½ x 8½, 128 pp, b/w illus., Quality PB, 978-1-893361-82-9 **$14.95**

The Sacred Art of Chant: Preparing to Practice
by Ana Hernández 5½ x 8½, 192 pp, Quality PB, 978-1-59473-036-8 **$15.99**

The Sacred Art of Fasting: Preparing to Practice
by Thomas Ryan, CSP 5½ x 8½, 192 pp, Quality PB, 978-1-59473-078-8 **$15.99**

The Sacred Art of Forgiveness: Forgiving Ourselves and Others through God's Grace
by Marcia Ford 8 x 8, 176 pp, Quality PB, 978-1-59473-175-4 **$16.99**

The Sacred Art of Listening: Forty Reflections for Cultivating a Spiritual Practice
by Kay Lindahl; Illustrations by Amy Schnapper
8 x 8, 160 pp, b/w illus., Quality PB, 978-1-893361-44-7 **$16.99**

The Sacred Art of Lovingkindness: Preparing to Practice
by Rabbi Rami Shapiro; Foreword by Marcia Ford
5½ x 8½, 176 pp, Quality PB, 978-1-59473-151-8 **$16.99**

Sacred Speech: A Practical Guide for Keeping Spirit in Your Speech
by Rev. Donna Schaper 6 x 9, 176 pp, Quality PB, 978-1-59473-068-9 **$15.99**
HC, 978-1-893361-74-4 **$21.95**

Meditation / Prayer

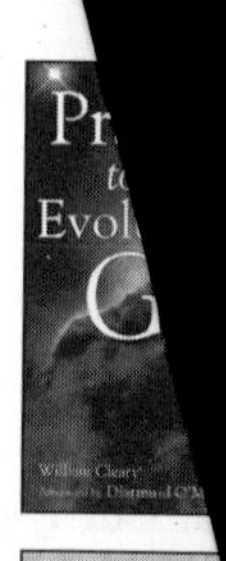

Prayers to an Evolutionary God

by William Cleary; Afterword by Diarmuid O'Murchu

How is it possible to pray when God is dislocated from heaven, dispersed all around us, and more of a creative force than an all-knowing father? Inspired by the spiritual and scientific teachings of Diarmuid O'Murchu and Teilhard de Chardin, Cleary reveals that religion and science can be combined to create an expanding view of the universe—an evolutionary faith.

6 x 9, 208 pp, HC, 978-1-59473-006-1 **$21.99**

Psalms: A Spiritual Commentary

by M. Basil Pennington, OCSO; Illustrations by Phillip Ratner

Showing how the Psalms give profound and candid expression to both our highest aspirations and our deepest pain, the late, highly respected Cistercian Abbot M. Basil Pennington shares his reflections on some of the most beloved passages from the Bible's most widely read book.

6 x 9, 176 pp, HC, 24 full-page b/w illus., 978-1-59473-141-9 **$19.99**

The Song of Songs: A Spiritual Commentary

by M. Basil Pennington, OCSO; Illustrations by Phillip Ratner

Join the late M. Basil Pennington as he ruminates on the Bible's most challenging mystical text. Follow a path into the Songs that weaves through his inspired words and the evocative drawings of Jewish artist Phillip Ratner—a path that reveals your own humanity and leads to the deepest delight of your soul.

6 x 9, 160 pp, HC, 14 b/w illus., 978-1-59473-004-7 **$19.99**

Women of Color Pray: Voices of Strength, Faith, Healing, Hope and Courage

Edited and with Introductions by Christal M. Jackson

Through these prayers, poetry, lyrics, meditations and affirmations, you will share in the strong and undeniable connection women of color share with God. It will challenge you to explore new ways of prayerful expression.

5 x 7¼, 208 pp, Quality PB, 978-1-59473-077-1 **$15.99**

The Art of Public Prayer: Not for Clergy Only

by Lawrence A. Hoffman

An ecumenical resource for all people looking to change hardened worship patterns.

6 x 9, 288 pp, Quality PB, 978-1-893361-06-5 **$18.99**

Finding Grace at the Center, 3rd Ed.: The Beginning of Centering Prayer
by M. Basil Pennington, OCSO, Thomas Keating, OCSO, and Thomas E. Clarke, SJ
Foreword by Rev. Cynthia Bourgeault, PhD
5 x 7¼, 128 pp, Quality PB, 978-1-59473-182-2 **$12.99**

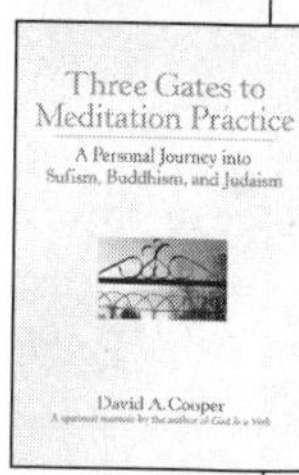

A Heart of Stillness: A Complete Guide to Learning the Art of Meditation
by David A. Cooper 5½ x 8½, 272 pp, Quality PB, 978-1-893361-03-4 **$16.95**

Meditation without Gurus: A Guide to the Heart of Practice
by Clark Strand 5½ x 8½, 192 pp, Quality PB, 978-1-893361-93-5 **$16.95**

Praying with Our Hands: 21 Practices of Embodied Prayer from the World's Spiritual Traditions *by Jon M. Sweeney; Photographs by Jennifer J. Wilson; Foreword by Mother Tessa Bielecki; Afterword by Taitetsu Unno, PhD*
8 x 8, 96 pp, 22 duotone photos, Quality PB, 978-1-893361-16-4 **$16.95**

Silence, Simplicity & Solitude: A Complete Guide to Spiritual Retreat at Home
by David A. Cooper 5½ x 8½, 336 pp, Quality PB, 978-1-893361-04-1 **$16.95**

Three Gates to Meditation Practice: A Personal Journey into Sufism, Buddhism, and Judaism *by David A. Cooper* 5½ x 8½, 240 pp, Quality PB, 978-1-893361-22-5 **$16.95**

Women Pray: Voices through the Ages, from Many Faiths, Cultures and Traditions
Edited and with Introductions by Monica Furlong
5 x 7¼, 256 pp, Quality PB, 978-1-59473-071-9 **$15.99**
Deluxe HC with ribbon marker, 978-1-893361-25-6 **$19.95**